# Guide to
# HISTORIC NEW BERN
## North Carolina

# Guide to
# HISTORIC NEW BERN,
# North Carolina

edited by
**DR. H. BRAUGHN TAYLOR**

Published by the New Bern/Craven County American Revolution Bicentennial Commission 1974

Front Cover: Armillary Sphere. This antique English copper Armillary Sphere on an English eighteenth century carved Purbeck stone pedestal was used in the study of astronomy. The time of day could be told by the shadow of the bar on the numbered rib or plate of the sphere, similar to a sundial. The Armillary Sphere is located in the Tryon Palace Garden.

Inside Front Cover: Silver Communion Service. King George II presented Christ Church this silver communion service in 1752, along with a Bible and a Prayer Book. The service is on display at Christ Church, and is still used regularly.

Inside Back Cover: Map of New Bern in 1769 drawn by C. J. Sauthier. The original is preserved at the North Carolina Division of Archives and History in Raleigh.

Back Cover: Aerial view of New Bern and the confluence of the Neuse River and Trent River looking eastward as the Neuse flows toward the Atlantic Ocean. This beautiful, broad expanse of water is the principal reason de Graffenried chose to settle here in 1710. The rivers have continued to nourish New Bern and to attract new residents ever since.

# TABLE OF CONTENTS

# GOVERNMENT AND BICENTENNIAL OFFICIALS

## New Bern Board of Aldermen

Charles H. Kimbrell, *Mayor*
Ben Hurst, *Mayor Pro Tem*
Mrs. Ella J. Bengel
Tom I. Davis
Gray Ingram
Tim Montgomery

## Craven County Board of Commissioners

Grover C. Lancaster, Jr., *Chairman*
Johnny E. Daugherty (deceased)
Sidney R. French, Jr.
R. Frank Hargett
Carmi E. Winters
J. W. Wynne, Jr.

## New Bern/Craven County-American Revolution Bicentennial Commission

Joseph M. Freemon, Jr., *Chairman*
George Allen Ives, Jr., *Vice-Chairman*
Mrs. Kathleen Orringer, *Secretary-Treasurer*
Rep. Chris Barker
Cedric M. Boyd (deceased)
Miss Gertrude Carraway
Mrs. Annie J. Gavin
Mrs. Carl S. Hagar
Mrs. Elinor D. Hawkins
Warren G. Keyes
Mrs. Grover C. Lancaster, Jr.
Miss Virginia McSorley
Mrs. Dale T. Millns
Tim Montgomery
Robert Lee Stallings, Jr.
Harold Talton
Carmi E. Winters

# INTRODUCTION

The Bicentennial observance of our nation's creation is a time for celebration and a time for reflection. It is a time for taking stock in where we are, and a time for anticipating where we are headed. New Bern and Craven County have chosen, quite properly, to celebrate the two-hundredth anniversary of an event that helped move the colonies toward independence. This event was the assembling in New Bern of the First Provincial Congress in August, 1774. This meeting was the first elected assembly in America to be called and held in defiance of royal authority. The resolutions and organization adopted by the First Provincial Congress represented the creation of the first revolutionary government in North Carolina. This book has been published as part of that observance.

The purposes of this book are many. One of the most important legacies a town can possess is the physical heritage of brick and mortar. One purpose of this volume is to pay tribute to the artisans and craftsmen, designers and builders of the historic buildings in our community. The talent and ability of those men who hand-crafted the mantel pieces and newel posts, and laid the brick in these buildings deserve to be praised and remembered, especially because these crafts have almost vanished. Secondly, it is easier to remember the people of the past and to comprehend their achievements if we can see where they lived and walk where they trod. The wood and brick of these buildings live because they contain the sweat and blood of the craftsmen who made them and the people who lived in them.

Fortunately in selecting the buildings to be featured in this book our task was made easier by the fact that the North Carolina Division of Archives and History had recently completed a survey of New Bern for the purpose of nominating entries for inclusion in the *National Register of Historic Places.* Over one-hundred forty structures were determined to be of sufficient historical and/or architectural value to be included. New Bern can indeed be proud to have so many of its buildings included in the *National Register.* This book pictures every one of these buildings that were still standing as of January, 1974. Unfortunately a few have been lost since the completion of the survey, and one major landmark was being destroyed as this book went to press.

A word needs to be said concerning the names of the buildings. We have followed in this volume the names used in the *National Register* whose policy is to designate a name when the building is entered on the *Register.* Those names are derived when the designer and/or original builder can be determined through scholarly research. A second, and sometimes third, name is included in the name of the building for the most historically significant person to live in the house. The practice of adding the name of the most recent occupant to the name of the house is confusing. When that practice has been followed, any change in ownership immediately makes all publications out-of-date. For anyone trying to do research, or trying to write about one of these buildings, it is a nightmare. Certainly those people who do live in these historic buildings deserve our unending gratitude for maintaining them. It is hoped that this publication and the entry of these buildings on the *National Register* will encourage the use of scholarly established names. It is also hoped that further research will be funded soon in order to determine the origin and history of every one of the buildings so they all can be given appropriate names.

One of the purposes of this volume is to encourage all of us to be more appreciative of our visual environment. The buildings in which we live and work affect our lives in more ways than simply providing shelter. Beautiful buildings should be a delight to the eyes and an inspiration to the spirit. Sometimes when we live too close to objects of beauty we take them for granted. It is hoped that this volume will remind us of our wealth of architectural beauty, and that it will encourage us to take the necessary steps to preserve this rich heritage for the generations who will live during our nation's next two-hundred years.

This book is by no means the work of one person. Several people have contributed in many ways. This volume would never have been published without the support of the sixteen members of the Bicentennial Commission, and especially of the Chairman, Joseph M. Freemon, Jr. The people who graciously opened their homes at times not always convenient to them deserve our appreciation. Most importantly, we should thank the man who did most of the black and white, and all of the color photography, Bob Jones of the Jones-Potts Music Company. Bob calls himself an amateur photographer. However, these pages will demonstrate that he is an artist of great talent. Nancy Springett spent many hours accompanying Bob and arranging for him to do the photography, and helped select the best pictures to use. This book would have been incomplete without Miss Gertrude Carraway's knowledgeable essay. Her wisdom and charm have been an inspiration. Janet K. Seapker's advice and professional judgment is reflected on almost every page. The staff of Tryon Palace, Michael Brantley, Donald Taylor, and Dabney Coddington, have given generously of their time and helpful suggestions. Emily Bunting's wise advice and patience has been a constant encouragement. Janet Latham came to our rescue at a crucial point with her calm professionalism. Mrs. Ellis Muther and Mary Pat Pelham, with expert artistic judgment, did the lay-out and design for the book on a very rushed schedule. And finally, Nelson Collins, Phil Killette and the craftsmen at Theo. Davis Sons, Inc., our printer, expertly translated our visions into a beautiful reality.

H. Braughn Taylor
Executive Director,
New Bern/Craven County
American Revolution
Bicentennial Commission

# HISTORICAL NOTES ON NEW BERN AND CRAVEN COUNTY

**By Gertrude Carraway**

After his 1660 restoration to the throne of England, King Charles II on March 24, 1663, issued a Carolina Charter granting to eight of his loyal supporters as Lords Proprietors wide areas in the New World spreading from Virginia to the Spanish line of Florida and from the Atlantic to the "South Seas" or the Pacific Ocean. This territory was practically the same which had been given by his father, King Charles I, to Sir Robert Heath and which had then been called "Carolina" for Carolus or Charles. By a second Charter June 30, 1665, Charles II extended the land limits to include what is now all or parts of fifteen states and northern Mexico.

One of the original Lords Proprietors was William, Earl of Craven (1608-1693), a brave soldier, who had assisted Charles II financially. When he died without lineal heirs, his share went to his grand-nephew, William Lord Craven, whose son of the same name and title next inherited it.

Bath Precinct was divided in 1705 into three precincts, one of them being named Archdale for the 1694-1696 Quaker Proprietary Governor of Carolina. About 1712 this was designated Craven Precinct, honoring William Lord Craven. The term precinct was changed in 1739 to county.

On December 7, 1710, Carolina was separated into North Carolina and South Carolina. Edward Hyde, Earl of Clarendon and cousin of Queen Anne of England, was appointed May 9, 1712, by the Lords Proprietors as the first Chief Executive of Albemarle, or North Carolina, independent of the government in South Carolina. Seven of the eight Lords Proprietors, including Lord Craven, in 1729 sold their Carolina interests to the British Crown. North Carolina thus became a Royal Colony, with its governors appointed by the King.

Early settlers drifted to this region. Some came directly from Europe, others from colonies to the north. French Huguenots under Pastor Phillips de Richebourg arrived in 1707 from a 1690 settlement in Virginia and colonized the other side of Trent River not far from the present location of New Bern. Before long they moved to South Carolina. Welsh Quakers settled during 1710 on Clubfoot and Hancock Creeks.

New Bern was founded in 1710 by German Palatines and Swiss colonists seeking religious and political freedom. Their leader was Baron Christopher DeGraffenried, a Swiss nobleman, born November 15, 1661. Although from Switzerland, he had spent much time in France and signed his name, "Christophle De Graffenried." Descendants continued to use the spelling of his surname but decapitalized and added the "de" to it as only one word. Queen Anne gave him encouragement and £4,200 in England to help start his colony here, which he named for his native city of Bern. From the aboriginal Indians be bought the land of "Chattawka," their name for their local village, said to mean "where the fish are taken out." It is reported that he laid out this town in the shape of a cross for two purposes: its religious significance and defense against the Indians.

Hardships developed. There was a scarcity of provisions and supplies. The newcomers were unaccustomed to the climate, and some succumbed to diseases. Aid failed to come, as expected, from abroad. DeGraffenried and Surveyor John Lawson were captured by Indians. The latter was burned at the stake, deGraffenried was spared. Taking advantage of internal strife and difficulties throughout North Carolina, the Indians laid secret plans for the destruction of the white intruders. After their disastrous "Great Massacre" during September 1711, their attacks were halted at Fort Barnwell in Craven County. When badly defeated in a decisive battle March 20-23, 1713, near Snow Hill, the Tuscaroras journeyed to upper New York, joining the Five Nations of Indians there and giving the name of their old village here, Chattawka, to their new home, now the world-famous Chautauqua, New York.

Discouraged and disillusioned, without funds or help, deGraffenried mortgaged the local lands to Col. Thomas Pollock, wealthy planter of the Chowan section and North Carolina's 1712-1714 Proprietary Governor. He then returned to Europe, arriving in Bern in December, 1713, and dying there on his eighty-second birthday in 1743.

By a 1715 Act of the Assembly North Carolina was divided into church parishes. "Neuse River and the branches thereof" were designated as the Parish of Craven. Another Assembly Act that year listed the places where residents were to vote. For Craven Parish there were two voting sites, "At New Bern town, so called, and Swift's Plantation." Despite hardships and dangers, New Bern and Craven Precinct grew and prospered. In 1723 New Bern was incorporated, made a Borough Town and the Precinct (County) Seat.

New Bern became rapidly Anglicized. Even its English pronunciation is still prevalent: NEW Bern, not New BERN. The last word is not spelled with a last "e". Berne is the French spelling. Bern, which means bear, is the German spelling. For centuries Switzerland has been predominantly German, and "Bern" is found there much more than "Berne". On the Plan of New Bern drafted in October, 1710, by Baron deGraffenried the name does not have a final "e". Nor does it when the town was incorporated. During the Civil War, after New Bern had fallen March 14, 1862, to Union troops commanded by Gen. Ambrose E. Burnside, Union soldiers added an "e" to New Bern. Following Reconstruction, at the insistence of local leaders, the General Assembly on February 20, 1899, officially fixed the spelling by law, as it had been originally: New Bern.

In the City Hall at Craven and Pollock Streets hangs a framed Bear Banner of Bern, presented February 27, 1896, by John B. Pioda, Swiss Ambassador to the United States, on behalf of the Bernese Council of Burghesses, after the Board of Aldermen two years previously had adopted the armorial bearing of the parent city. This is a rare instance of an American city owning a City Flag donated by the European capital for which it is named. Three black copper bears, as symbols of the town, were bought in 1914 and attached to the Old City Hall on lower Craven Street. Upon the construction of a new Federal Building on Middle and New Streets, the City Hall was moved to the 1897-1935 Federal Building and two of the bears were attached there. The third bear was put in a niche at the top of the facade of the Central Fire Station on Broad Street. Carrying out the "bear" significance, athletic teams here have long been dubbed "Bears", "Bruins," or "Cubs." Inside the City Hall are a number of recent gifts from Bern. There, too, are old parchment grants to deGraffenried, who was honored with the title of "Landgrave of Carolina and Baron of Bernburg." This is the only town in the country to have had a founder with a title of nobility bestowed for America.

Craven County is one of the largest counties in the State, but it is much smaller than it was at first. Five other counties have been formed from it, and parts of it have been transferred to three other

*Council Bluff: (East Front and Broad Streets). Baron de Graffenried is believed to have landed near here with his band of settlers in 1710.*

nearby counties. The earliest registers extant at the Craven County Court House cover six counties. Records of grants and deeds date back to 1703. The first will book begins in 1713, with a continuous sequence. Entries of vacant lands can be traced from 1728. The court docket begins in 1746; land patents begin in 1772.

New Bern became the largest town in colonial North Carolina and the center of business and political activity. The Governor's Council, or Upper House of the Assembly, met here frequently, as early as 1737. The assembly held at least thirty-three sessions in New Bern, more than at any other place, from 1739 until December 5, 1770, when it convened for the first time in the new Colonial Capitol, now known as Tryon Palace.

While Royal Governor William Tryon was the first resident executive in the Palace, the Council from October, 1770, through June, 1771, had twenty-three meetings in its Council Chamber. It met there in each of those nine months except May, 1771, when Tryon was busy upstate during the War of the Regulation. For more than a month the Lower House also met in New Bern.

Royal Governor Josiah Martin met with the Council seven times and with the Lower House five times while he resided in the Palace. He angrily dissolved the last Assembly under the Crown on April 8, 1775, because, overriding his stern objection, for five previous days the Second Provincial Convention or Congress had been meeting in this city. Martin, North Carolina's last Royal Governor, fled from New Bern in May, 1775, the first Royal Governor to be exiled from any of the thirteen American colonies. The first State General Assembly met April 7-May 9, 1777, and held seven other sessions at intervals in New Bern until July, 1794, five months before it began to meet regularly in the new Capital City of Raleigh.

Due to its unique distinction as government house and governor's residence, the Palace, Colonial Capitol and first State Capitol, is the only building where Royal and State Governors lived, began administrative terms, met with legislatures, and performed other official duties. Two Royal Governors, James Hasell and Josiah Martin, took their Oaths of Office in the Palace. Four State

Governors, Richard Caswell, Abner Nash, Alexander Martin and Richard Dobbs Spaight, Sr., also were installed or inaugurated there.

In March, 1951, the General Assembly held a short, special meeting in New Bern during its biennial session. For the official opening of the Tryon Palace Restoration on April 8, 1959, both Houses of the Assembly met in the restored Palace and the Legislators, State Officials, Supreme Court Justices and their wives were lavishly entertained in the city. A few days later the British and Swiss Ambassadors to the United States here honored guests at other gala programs sponsored by the Tryon Palace Commission.

Long known as "The Athens of North Carolina," because of its historical, cultural and educational attainments, New Bern was the home of James Davis, who came from Virginia in 1749 as North Carolina's first printer. Here he set up the first printing press of the province and published its first newspaper, first pamphlet and first book.

The first book store in the State was opened here in 1783 by Robert Keith and Francis Xavier Martin, printers and editors. Martin was the first Postmaster of the first postoffice in North Carolina which opened here June 1, 1790. He was the Representative from the Borough Town of New Bern in the 1806 House of Commons, and became a prominent historian and jurist. For thirty-one years he was on the Louisiana State Supreme Court, ten of those years as Chief Justice.

Through the influence of the Rev. James Reed, first regular rector of Christ Episcopal Church, the first school in the province was opened here January 1, 1764, by his assistant, Thomas Tomlinson. Under a bill introduced by Col. Joseph Leech, the Assembly ratified March 9th an "Act for building a schoolhouse and schoolmaster's residence in New Bern." Reed, Leech, John Williams, Thomas Haslen, Thomas Clifford Howe, Richard Fenner and Richard Cogdell were named the school's first trustees. Williams was a Justice of the Peace. Haslen became Mayor; Leech, Mayor and one of the first

Union Point: (East Front Street at Tryon Palace Drive). Location selected by de Graffenried for the first Government House. The land was purchased by him from Indian Chief, King Taylor.

Councillors of State; Howe, an Assemblyman; Fenner, Recorder of the Borough Town of New Bern; and Cogdell, Alderman, Sheriff, State Legislator and State Treasurer. This was the first incorporated school in North Carolina and the second private secondary school in English America to receive a charter. Following interruptions during the Revolutionary War, the school was reorganized as the New Bern Academy by the 1784 Assembly. The nine men appointed on its first School Board were former Governors Caswell and Nash; Spaight, who signed the Federal Constitution and was the 1792-1795 Governor; William Blount, also a Constitution Signer, later becoming Governor of the Territory South of the River Ohio and Senator from Tennessee; John Wright Stanly, illustrious patriot, who lost fourteen privateers during the Revolution; John Sitgreaves, member of Continental Congress and afterwards Speaker of the House and Federal Judge; Brig. Gen. William Bryan, delegate to three Provincial Congresses and Assemblyman, who had taken a gallant part in the Battle of Moore's Creek Bridge; Maj. Gen. William McClure, Revolutionary surgeon; and Sypers Singleton, scholarly soldier, who played a vital role in the famed case of Bayard versus Singleton here in 1786 when it was held for the first time by an American Court that a legislature is limited in power by a constitution.

North Carolina's first free school was started here in 1798 by Dr. William Hawes. From a bequest of Moses Griffin, one of the first free trade schools for orphan girls, if not the first, was opened in New Bern. During the Civil War Occupation the first Negro schools in the State were established here by Northerners, under the guidance of Vincent Colyer, Superintendent of the Poor in this Capital City of the Federal Department of North Carolina. As one of the four Negro Normal Schools created by the 1881 State Legislature, along with four such schools for whites, a Negro Normal School, headed by Ella W. Sommerville, existed here through 1887.

Countless New Bernians have been outstanding in all fields of public service and private enterprise. Courageous military officers have ranked high on the battle fronts; other citizens have been patriotic workers on the home fronts. Some attained prominence along literary and cultural lines; many others in religious, educational, industrial, professional and political circles. Although impossible to print a complete Roll of Honor, a few examples in addition to those already mentioned, should be cited.

Ministers of practically all the local churches achieved fame not only as theologians but also as educators. Pastors of the First Baptist Church served as college presidents, school principals and denominational editors. Several were instrumental in the founding and early direction of Wake Forest University. Thomas Meredith started *The Biblical Recorder* here on January 5, 1835, and his name was given to Meredith College. Furman University was named for another pastor, Richard Furman, Jr. John Nicholson Campbell, a supply Presbyterian pastor, left here to be Chaplain of Congress. Drury Lacy, a pastor of the First Presbyterian Church, was President of Davidson College and he and his wife opened a Raleigh school which became Peace College. Dr. Charles G. Vardell, another Presbyterian pastor, was the first President of Flora Macdonald College. Jonathan Otis Freeman, M. D., Presbyterian minister, while Principal of the New Bern Academy was aided in the school by his brother, George W. Freeman, who was elected the Episcopal Bishop of Arkansas. Alfred A. Watson, a rector of Christ Church, became the first Bishop of the Diocese of East Carolina. Thomas P. Irving was one of the town's first educators; as was Solomon Halling, M. D., a Revolutionary War Surgeon. Both were rectors of Christ

Church. Though not local rectors, two native New Bernians were distinguished clergymen. Francies Lister Hawks, D.D., LL.D., eminent orator, educator and historian. Three times declining Bishoprics, he was the first President of the University of Louisiana. His brother, Cicero Stephen Hawks, was the first Episcopal Bishop of Missouri. Sons of Francis Hawks, who succeeded Maj. John Daves as the first two Collectors of Customs here, they were grandsons of John Hawks, supervising architect of the original Tryon Palace and the State's first Auditor.

Innumerable other laymen have been active in religious and educational leadership. Dr. David Bancroft Johnson, local school superintendent, was the founder and first President of Winthrop College. Stephen D. Pool, local newspaper editor, was the 1874-1876 State Superintendent of Public Instruction. Samuel M. Brinson of the First Baptist Church was a Congressman from 1919 until his death in 1922.

Thomas Tomlinson bequeathed money in 1802 to Christ Church for the opening of a library here. A New Bern Library Company flourished during the early portion of the nineteenth century. Miss Caroline Durand Mayhew in 1890 started at King's Daughters public library, taken over by Miss Leah Jones (later Mrs. Charles L. Stevens), which was the forerunner of the current New Bern-Craven County Public Library.

Three New Bern citizens were Governors of North Carolina: Abner Nash, Richard Dobbs Spaight, Sr., and R. D. Spaight, Jr. Two former residents were also Governors: Richard Caswell and Benjamin Williams. Two Governors, W. A. Graham and J. W. Ellis, were married here to New Bern ladies.

Martin Howard was on the Royal Governors' Council, 1770-1776, and served as the 1767-1776 Chief Justice. John Louis Taylor, a former New Bernian, was the first Chief Justice of the State Supreme Court; and Frederick Nash, a native New Bernian, was later Chief Justice. William Gaston and Matthias E. Manly were Associate Justices. Gaston, born here, was also a State Representative, State Senator, Congressman, champion of religious liberty, and the author of the State Song. Manly was a local postmaster, State Representative and Senator, and Superior Court Judge. Sixteen residents or former residents were Superior Court Judges, and four were Federal Judges. George E. Badger, born in New Bern, was Secretary of the Navy, United States Senator and Superior Court Judge. Furnifold M. Simmons was a Congressman two years and a United States Senator thirty years, longer than any other Tar Heel. Nineteen New Bernians and a former New Bernian have served in Congress.

Nine New Bernians were Councillors of State, including Dr. Isaac Guion, Revolutionary surgeon and State Legislator, and Marquis de Bretigny, who had commanded North Carolina Cavalry at the Battle of Guilford Courthouse. Charles R. Thomas, Sr. was North Carolina's Secretary of State and, like his namesake son, went to Congress. Numerous citizens have been Colonial and State Assemblymen. Twelve were Speakers of the State House; Abner Nash, James Coor and M. E. Manly were State Senate Speakers. Nash died while in the Continental Congress; Coor served one term in the State House and eleven terms in the State Senate.

Natives achieving diversified fame elsewhere include Edward Stanly, Speaker of the State House, State Attorney General and Congressman; and Hannis Taylor, Minister to Spain and an authority on International Law. Among many other noteworthy personages were Samuel Cornell, prosperous Tory merchant here, who lent money for the erection of the original Tryon Palace, a granddaughter being Daniel Webster's second wife and another descendant founding Cornell University; and James Johnston Pettigrew, a youthful resident, killed in 1863 while a heroic Confederate General.

Inventors born in New Bern include Gen. Gabriel J. Rains, whose submarine explosives kept Federal fleets at bay; his brother, Gen. George W. Rains, who made the torpedoes effective through fuse priming and obtained steam engine patents; and Dr. Frederick D. Lente, who invented an early instrument for blood transfusions. At his shop here in 1829 John Gill, locksmith and silversmith, made a revolver, a percussion weapon with fourteen chambers, said to be the first of its kind.

Three Presidents of the United States visited New Bern: George Washington, James Monroe and Harry Truman. Two early Methodist divines, Joseph Pilmoor and George Whitefield, preached here. Among other noted visitors were Sir William Draper, "Conqueror of Manila"; Don Francisco deMiranda, "the precurser of the Independence Movement in Spanish America", and Edward Everett, famous orator.

Besides those previously listed, New Bern claims many other priorities: first in America to observe Washington's Birthday; first in North Carolina and third in America to celebrate Independence Day; first postal service in the region; first steam sawmill; first macadamized road and brick highways in the region; first public banking institutions and one of the first two chartered banks in North Carolina; first Salvation Army in North or South Carolina; first large four-faced clock on a building; first railroad 100 percent diesel-operated; first motion picture theater built from the ground up; one of the first ships and the first modern naval minesweeper built and launched in the State.

New Bern has the oldest theater in America still in regular operation; oldest school building still in use in North Carolina; oldest benevolent society still functioning in the State and perhaps second oldest in the United States; oldest fire company of the State with its earliest charter extant; oldest Roman Catholic parish in North Carolina; oldest Christian Science Church in East Carolina; oldest Presbyterian organization and sanctuary in the Presbytery; and one of the oldest Episcopal parishes in the South.

This city was one of the first towns of its size to own its electric light plant and start rural electrification and one of the first places in the State to open a public library, form a mutual fire insurance company, and establish a pulp mill. One of the first ten United States Coast Guard Cutters and one of the first gasoline buggy-automobiles were built here. Here was organized the first Community Council to aid unemployed and needy persons. A canal cut by Indians from the mouth of Neuse River to Core Sound was one of the first internal improvements in Carolina. The first road and first ferry in North Carolina led from New Bern to Bath. One of the "twenty most historic trees in the country" is here. Local firemen broke a number of world records. New Bern is one of the smallest cities in the world to confer all Masonic degrees except the 33rd, including the Shrine.

Twenty-two State Historical Highway Markers have been erected in Craven County and sixty-seven sites of interest have been marked in the city, termed "Treasure Town of Exquisite Architecture." New Bern has twenty-four homes enrolled in the *National Register of Historic Places*. In that *Register* are two homes elsewhere in the county, six local churches, City Hall, Masonic Temple, Central School, Cedar Grove Cemetery and Baxter Clock. So many structures qualified that they were combined in a 38th classification: "New Bern Historic District."

North Carolina

At a general meeting of Deputies of the Inhabitants of this Province at NewBern the 25th Day of August Anno Dom 1774.

We His Majesty's most dutiful and Loyal Subjects, the Deputies from the Several Counties and Towns of the Province of North Carolina, impressed with the most sacred respect for the British Constitution, and Resolved to maintain the Succession of the House of Hanover as by Law Established, and avowing our inviolable and unshaken Fidelity to our Sovereign, and entertaining a sincere regard for our fellow Subjects in Great Britain, Viewing with the utmost abhorrence every attempt which may tend to disturb the peace and good order of this Colony, or to shake the Fidelity of His Majesty's Subjects resident here, but at the same time Conceiving it a duty which we owe to ourselves and posterity, in the present alarming state of British America, when our most essential rights are invaded by Powers unwarrantable assumed by the Parliament of Great Britain, to declare our Sentiments in the most public Manner, lest our Silence should be Construed as Acquiescence; and that we patiently submit to the Burthen which they have thought fit to impose upon us.

Resolved that His Majesty George the Third is lawful and rightful King of Great-Britain, and the Dominions thereunto belonging, and of this Province as part thereof, and that we do bear faithful and true allegiance unto him as our lawful Sovereign, and that we will to the utmost of our power maintain and Defend the Succession of the House of Hanover as by Law Established against the open or private attempts of any person or power whatsoever.

Resolved that we claim no more than the rights of Englishmen without Diminution or abridgment, That it is our indispensible duty, and will be our Constant endeavour to maintain those rights to the utmost of our Power Consistently with the Loyalty which we owe our Sovereign, and a Sacred

# THE JOURNAL OF THE PROCEEDINGS OF THE FIRST PROVINCIAL CONVENTION OR CONGRESS OF NORTH CAROLINA, HELD AT NEWBERN ON THE TWENTY-FIFTH DAY OF AUGUST, A.D. 1774.

North Carolina—Ss.

At a General meeting of Deputies of the Inhabitants of this province at Newbern the twenty-fifth day of August in the year of our Lord one thousand seven hundred and seventy four

Appeared for

Anson County—Samuel Spencer, William Thomas. Beaufort—Roger Ormond, Thomas Respess. Bladen—William Salter, Walter Gibson. Bute—William Person, Green Hill. Brunswick—Robert Howe. Bertie—John Campbell. Craven—Lemuel Hatch, Joseph Leech, Richard Cogdell. Carteret—William Thomson, Solomon Perkins. Currituck—Nathan Joyner, Samuel Jarvis. Chowan—Samuel Johnston, Thomas Oldham, Thomas Benbury, Thomas Jones, Thomas Hunter. Cumberland—Ferquard Campbell, Thomas Rutherford. Chatham—Richard Caswell, William McKinnie. Dobbs—George Miller, Simon Bright, Thomas Gray, Thomas Hix. Duplin—James Kenan, William Dickson. Edgecombe— Granville—Thomas Person, Memucan Hunt. Guilford— Hyde—Rothias Latham, Samuel Smith. Hertford— Halifax—Nicholas Long, Willie Jones. Johnston—Needham Bryan, Benjamin Williams. Mecklenburg—Benjamin Patten. Martin—Edmund Smythwick. New Hanover—John Ashe, William Hooper. Northampton—Allen Jones. Orange—Thomas Hart. Onslow— William Cray, John Harvey, Benjamin Harvey. Perquimans—Andrew Knox, Thomas Harvey, John Whedbee, Jr., Joseph Jones. Pasquotank—Edward Everigin, Joseph Reading. Pitt—John Simpson, Edward Salter, William Kenon. Rowan—Moses Winslow, Samuel Young. Surry— Tryon—David Jenkins, Robert Alexander. Tyrell—Joseph Spruill, Jeremiah Fraiser. Wake— Newbern—Abner Nash, Isaac Edwards. Edenton—Joseph Hewes. Wilmington—Francis Clayton. For the Town of Bath—Mr. William Brown. For the Town of Halifax—Mr. John Geddy. For the Town of Hillsborough—          For the Town of Salisbury— William Kennon. For the Town of Brunswick— For the Town of Campbelton—

The deputies then proceeded to make choice of a moderator, when Col. John Harvey was unanimously chosen and Mr. Andrew Knox appointed clerk.

The meeting adjourned till 8 o'clock tomorrow morning.

## Friday August 26th 1774.

The meeting met according to adjournment.

Mr. Hewes one of the members of the Committee of Correspondence presented several letters from the Committees of Correspondence of the other Colonies in America, and the several answers thereto, which on motion were ordered to be read, and after the most mature deliberations had thereon,

Resolved that three delegates be appointed to attend the General Congress to be held at Philadelphia sometime in September next.

The meeting adjourned till 8 o'clock tomorrow morning.

## Saturday August 27th 1774

The meeting met according to Adjournment and came to the following resolutions, to wit,

We his Majesty's most dutiful and Loyal Subjects, the deputies from the several Counties and Towns, of the Province of North Carolina, impressed with the most sacred respect for the British Constitution, and resolved to maintain the succession of the House of Hanover, as by law Established, and avowing our inviolable and unshaken Fidelity to our soverign, and entertaining a sincere regard for our fellow subjects in Great Britain viewing with the utmost abhorrence every attempt which may tend to disturb the peace and good order of this Colony, or to shake the fidelity of his Majesty's subjects resident here, but at the same time conceiving it a duty which we owe to ourselves and to posterity, in the present alarming state of British America, when our most essential rights are invaded by powers unwarrantably assumed by the Parliament of Great Britain to declare our sentiments in the most public manner, lest silence should be construed as acquiescence, and that we patiently submit to the Burdens which they have thought fit to impose upon us.

Resolved, That His Majesty George the third is lawful and rightful King of Great Britain, and the dominions thereunto belonging, and of this province as part thereof, and that we do bear faithful and true allegiance unto him as our lawful soverign, that we will to the utmost of our power, maintain and defend the succession of the House of Hanover as by law established against the open or private attempts of any person or persons whatsoever.

Resolved, That we claim no more than the rights of Englishmen, without diminution or abridgement, that it is our indispensable duty and will be our constant endeavour, to maintain those rights to the utmost of our power consistently with the loyalty which we owe our soverign, and sacred regard for the British Constitution.

Resolved That it is the very essence of the British Constitution that no subject should be taxed but by his own consent, freely given by himself in person or by his legal representatives, and that any other than such a taxation is highly derogatory to the rights of a subject and a gross violation of the grand charter of our liberties.

Resolved, That as the British subjects resident in North America, have nor can have any representation in the Parliament of Great Britain, Therefore any act of Parliament imposing a tax is illegal and unconstitutional, That our Provincial Assemblies, the King by his governors constituting one branch thereof, solely and exclusively possess that right.

Resolved, That the duties imposed by several acts of the British Parliament, upon Tea and other articles consumed in America for the purpose of raising a revenue, are highly illegal and oppressive, and that the late Exportation of tea by the East India Company to different parts of America was intended to give effect to one of the said Acts and thereby establish a precedent highly dishonorable to America and to obtain an implied assent to the powers which Great Britain had unwarrantably assumed of levying a tax upon us without our consent.

Resolved, That the inhabitants of the Massachusetts province have distinguished themselves in a manly support of the rights of America in general and that the cause in which they suffer is the Cause of every honest American who deserves the Blessings which the Constitution holds forth to them. That the Grievances under which the town of Boston labours at present are the effect of a resentment levelled at them for having stood foremost in an opposition to measures which must eventually involve all British America in a state of abject dependence and servitude.

The act of Parliament commonly called the Boston Port Act, as it tends to shut up the Port of Boston and thereby effectually destroy its Trade and deprive the Merchants and Manufacturers of a subsistance which they have hitherto procured by an honest industry, as it takes away the Wharves, Quays and other property of many individuals, by rendering it useless to them, and as the duration of this Act depends upon Circumstances founded merely in opinion, and in their nature indeterminate, and thereby may make the miseries it carries with it even perpetual,

Resolved therefore that it is the most cruel infringement of the rights and privileges of the people of Boston, both as men, and members of the British Government.

Resolved, That the late Act of Parliament for regulating the Police of that province is an infringement of the Charter right granted them by their Majesties, King William and Queen Mary, and tends to lessen that sacred confidence which ought to be placed in the Acts of Kings.

Resolved, That trial by Juries of the vicinity is the only lawful inquest that can pass upon the life of a British subject and that it is a right handed down to us from the earliest stages confirmed and sanctified by Magna Charta itself that no freeman shall be taken and imprisoned or dispossessed of his free tenement and Liberties or outlawed or banished or otherwise hurt or injured unless by the legal judgment of his peers or by the law of the Land, and therefore all who suffer otherwise are not victims to public justice but fall a sacrifice to the powers of Tyranny and highhanded oppression.

Resolved, That the Bill for altering the administration of justice in certain criminal cases, within the province of Massachusetts Bay as it empowers the Governors thereof to send to Great Britain for trial all persons who in aid of his Majestys officers shall commit any capital offence is fraught with the highest injustice and partiality and will tend to produce frequent bloodshed of its inhabitants, as this act furnishes an opportunity to commit the most atrocious Crimes with the Greatest probability of impunity.

Resolved, That we will not directly or indirectly after the first day of January 1775 import from Great Britain any East India Goods or any merchandize whatever, medicines excepted, nor will we after that day import from the West Indies or elsewhere any East India or British Goods or Manufactures, nor will we purchase any such articles so imported of any person or persons whatsoever, except such as are now in the Country or may arrive on or before the first day of January 1775.

Resolved, That unless American Grievances are redressed before the first day of October 1775, We will not after that day directly or indirectly export Tobacco, Pitch, Tar, Turpentine, or any other article whatsoever, to Great Britain, nor will we sell any such articles as we think can be exported to Great Britain, with a prospect of Gain to any Person or Persons whatever with a design of putting it in his or their power to export the same to Great Britain either on our own, his, or their account.

Resolved, That we will not import any slave or slaves, nor purchase any slave or slaves imported or brought into this province by others from any part of the world after the first day of November next.

Resolved, That we will not use nor suffer East India Tea to be used in our Families after the tenth day of September next, and that we will consider all persons in this province not complying with this resolve to be enemies of their Country.

Resolved, That the Venders of Merchandize within this province ought not to take advantage of the Resolves relating to non importation in this province or elsewhere but ought to sell their Goods or Merchandize which they have or may hereafter import, at the same rates they have been accustomed to sell them within three months last past.

Resolved, That the people of this province will break off all trade, Commerce, and dealings, and will not maintain any, the least trade, dealing or Commercial intercourse, with any Colony on this Continent, or with any city or town, or with any individual in such Colony, City or town, which shall refuse, decline, or neglect to adopt and carry into execution such General plan, as shall be agreed to in the Continental Congress.

Resolved, That we approve of the proposal of a General Congress to be held in the City of Philadelphia, on the 20th of September next, then and there to deliberate upon the present state of British America and to take such measures as they may deem prudent to effect the purpose of describing with certainty the Rights of Americans, repairing the breaches made in those rights and for guarding them for the future from any such violations done under the sanction of public authority.

Resolved, That William Hooper, Joseph Hewes and Richard Caswell Esquires, and every of them be Deputies to attend such Congress, and they are hereby invested with such powers as may make any Act done by them or consent given in behalf of this province Obligatory in honor upon every inhabitant thereof who is not an alien to his Country's good and an apostate to the liberties of America.

Resolved, That they view the attempt made by the ministers upon the Town of Boston, as a prelude to a general attack upon the rights of the other Colonies, and that upon the success of this depends in a great measure the Happiness of America, in its present race and in posterity and that therefore it becomes our duty to Contribute in proportion to our abilities to ease the burden imposed upon that town for their Virtuous Opposition to the Revenue Acts that they may be enabled to persist in a prudent and Manly opposition to the schemes of Parliament and render its dangerous design abortive.

Resolved, That Liberty is the Spirit of the British Constitution, and that it is the duty, and will be the Endeavour of us as British Americans to transmit this happy Constitution to our posterity in a state if possible better than we found it, and to suffer it to undergo a change which may impair that invaluable Blessing would be to disgrace those ancestors who at the Expense of their blood purchased those privileges which their degenerate posterity are too weak or too wicked to maintain inviolate.

Resolved, That every future provincial meeting when any division shall happen the method to be observed shall be to vote by the Counties and Towns (having a right to send members to Assembly) that shall be represented at every such meeting; and it is recommended to the deputies of the several Counties, That a Committee of five persons be chosen in each County by such persons as acceed to this association to take effectual care that these Resolves be properly observed and to correspond occasionally with the Provincial Committee of Correspondence of this province.

Resolved, That each and every County in this Province raise as speedily as possible the sum of twenty pounds Proclamation money and pay the same into the hands of Richard Caswell Esquire, to be by him equally divided among the Deputies appointed to attend the General Congress at Philadelphia as a recompense for their trouble and expense in attending the said Congress.

Resolved, That the moderator of this meeting and in case of his death Samuel Johnston Esquire be impowered on any future occasion that may in his opinion require it to convene the several deputies of this province which now are or hereafter shall be chosen, at such time and place as he shall think proper, or in case of the death or absence of any deputy it is recommended that another be chosen in his stead.

Resolved, That the following instructions for the deputies appointed to meet in General Congress on the part of this Colony to wit: That they express their most sincere attachment to our most gracious sovereign King George the third, and our determined resolution to support his Lawful authority in this Province, at the same time we cannot depart from a steady adherence to the first law of Nature, a firm and resolute defence of our persons and properties against all unconstitutional encroachments whatever.

That they assert our rights to all the privileges of British subjects particularly that of paying no taxes or duties but with our own consent, and that the Legislature of this province, have the exclusive power of making laws to regulate our internal Polity subject to his Majesty's disallowance.

That should the British Parliament continue to exercise the power of levying taxes and duties on the Colonies, and making laws to bind them in all cases whatsoever; such laws must be highly unconstitutional, and oppressive to the inhabitants of British America, who have not, and from their local circumstances cannot have a fair and equal representation in the British Parliament, and that these disadvantages must be greatly enhanced by the misrepresentation of designing Men inimical to the Colonies, the influence of whose reports cannot be guarded against, by reason of the distance of America from them or as has been unhapily experienced in the case of the Town of Boston, when the ears of the administration have been shut, against every attempt to vindicate a people, who claimed only the right of being heard in their own defence.

That therefore until we obtain an explicit declaration and acknowledgment of our rights, we agree to stop all imports, from Great Britain after the first day of January 1775, and that we will not export any of our Commodities to Great Britain after the first day of October 1775.

That they concur with the Deputies or Delegates from the other Colonies, in such regulation, address or remonstrance, as may be deemed most probable to restore a lasting harmony, and good understanding with Great Britain, a circumstance we most sincerely and ardently desire and that they agree with a majority of them in all necessary measures, for promoting a redress of such grievances as may come under their consideration.

Resolved, That the thanks of this meeting be given to the Hon. John Harvey Esquire Moderator for his faithful exercise of that office and the services he has thereby rendered to this Province and the Friends of America in General.

JOHN HARVEY, Moderator.

| | | | |
|---|---|---|---|
| | | | Simon Bright |
| Richard Cogdell | Edward Everigin | Sam. Smith | Thos Gray |
| Wm Thomson | Edward Salter | Willie Jones | Thos Hicks |
| Solomon Perkins | Sam. Young | Benj. Patten | James Kenan |
| Nathan Joyner | Joseph Spruil | Allen Jones | William Dickson |
| Sam. Jarvis | Joseph Hewes | Benj. Harvey | Thos. Person |
| Sam. Johnston | John Geddy | J. Whedbee | Rothias Latham |
| Thos. Benbury | Sam Spencer | Joseph Reading | Needham Bryan |
| Thos. Jones | Wm Thomas | Wm Kennon | John Ashe |
| Thos. Oldham | Roger Ormond | David Jenkins | Thomas Hart |
| Thos. Hunter | Thos. Respess, Jr | Abner Nash | Andrew Knox |
| Ferqd Campbell | Wm Salter | Francis Clayton | Joseph Jones |
| M. Hunt | Walter Gibson | Edward Smythwick | John Simpson |
| Nick Long | Wm Person | Lemuel Hatch | Moses Winslow |
| Benj. Williams | Green Hill | Thomas Rutherford | Robert Alexander |
| William Hooper | R. Howe | R. Caswell | I. Edwards |
| Wm Cray | John Campbell | Wm McKinnie | William Brown |
| Thos. Harvey | James Coor | Geo. Miller | Jeremiah Frasier |

# NORTH CAROLINA'S FIRST PROVINCIAL CONGRESS IN HISTORICAL PERSPECTIVE

**By H. Braughn Taylor**

The summer of 1774 was a crucial time for British-Americans. For ten years the colonies in America had been arguing with the mother country over imperial policy and the basic rights of Englishmen. The struggle had begun in the aftermath of the Great War For Empire, 1754-1763. In that conflict, Great Britain had emerged as the strongest international power in Europe. She had pushed France off the North American continent and had more than doubled the size of her American empire by adding Canada and the eastern half of the Mississippi Valley. Great Britain at the end of the war in 1763, stood as the unchallenged master of European civilization. Yet reaching that position had proved very expensive. The National Debt of Britain in 1763 reached £130 million, double what it had been in 1754. In addition, the cost of administering her greatly enlarged empire had risen from £70,000 a year in 1748, to over £350,000 a year in 1764.

To the men responsible for governing Great Britain, it seemed only natural that the British living in North America should help pay for the increased cost of administering the empire. To implement that policy, Parliament passed the American Revenue Act in 1764, and the Stamp Act in 1765. The Revenue Act, or "Sugar Act", actually lowered custom duties on the importation of sugar products from the French West Indies. The Stamp Act, similar to a law already operative in England, provided for revenue stamps to be affixed to all newspapers, almanacs, pamphlets, legal documents of all types, insurance policies, ships' papers, and even dice and playing cards. The money raised by these stamp duties was to be used solely for the purpose of "defending, protecting, and securing the colonies." Offenses against the law were to be tried in Admiralty Courts, in which juries were not used. This was the first direct tax ever to be levied on the colonies by Parliament, the first tax of any sort other than custom duties.

The reaction in America was swift and decisive opposition. In colony after colony respectable men, organized as "Sons of Liberty", forced stamp officers to resign their positions and burned the unsold stamps. In several colonies mobs attacked royal officials and forced the courts to close. The worst violence took place in New York, Boston, Philadelphia, Annapolis, and Charleston. The Stamp Act was completely nullified by violence and none of the stamps were used. In addition to using force and the threat of force to nullify royal policy, the merchants in several colonies joined together and resolved to use economic pressure on Parliament by refusing to import articles from Great Britain.

The most important American response to the Stamp Act was the assembling of the Stamp Act Congress in October, 1765. This was the first inter-colonial meeting to be summoned by American initiative. At the Stamp Act Congress and in political pamphlets published at the time, new political theories were developed. The Americans believed that Parliament had no right to tax the colonies because the colonies were not represented in Parliament: "No taxation without representation." Each colony, they believed, had in its own Assembly a miniature Parliament, and that only these assemblies could tax the colonies.

North Carolina, (along with New Hampshire, Virginia, and Georgia), was not represented at the Stamp Act Congress, because Governor Tryon refused to assemble the legislature in time to elect delegates. Nevertheless, North Carolina did resist the Stamp Act, most significantly by using armed mobs at Wilmington to force Stamp Officer William Houston to resign his position, and when armed Sons of Liberty prevented Governor Tryon from enforcing the Act.

In England the protests of the Americans had their desired effect. Parliament, encouraged by King George III, repealed the Stamp Act in March, 1766. The law was repealed because it could not be enforced against unified opposition, and because English merchants and manufacturers suffered from the boycott of British goods which had been organized by the Sons of Liberty. However, Parliament did not give up its right to tax the colonies. After repealing the Stamp Act it passed the Declaratory Act which affirmed Parliament's right, as the sovereign legislature of the empire, to make laws binding the colonies "in all cases whatsoever."

In 1767 Parliament passed the Townshend Acts, believing that if the colonists would not accept an internal tax, they would pay customs duties. The Townshend Acts levied import duties on glass, lead, paints, paper and tea imported into the colonies. The colonists objected to these duties just as strenuously as they had opposed the Stamp Act. One aspect of the Townshend Acts, however, was more alarming to the Americans than the mere fact that these were taxes levied without their consent. The most disturbing feature of the Townshend Acts was the use to which the money raised by them was to be put. The Townshend Duties revenue was to be used to pay the salaries of colonial officials.

This failure to finance a colonial civil list is one of the most difficult to understand features of the British empire in the eighteenth century. Especially puzzling was the failure to pay out of royal income the salaries of judges and governors. These officials' salaries were usually supplied by a fee system. Each governor was instructed by the Crown to obtain his salary from the legislature of his colony. This put the governors in an impossible position and gave the legislatures of the colonies more power than the Crown desired. It was the proposal to pay the salaries of governors and judges from the revenue raised by the Townshend Duties that alarmed the colonists more than anything else. If the judges and governors were made independent of the legislatures, there would be no way for the colonists to evade or defy the will of Great Britain as they had been able to do in many areas for decades.

Because non-importation appeared to have forced Parliament to repeal the Stamp Act, many merchants again in 1768 and 1769 swore not to import British goods in an attempt to force repeal of the Townshend Duties. Non-importation cut in half the value of goods imported from Britain. Again the economic weapon seemed to work, for in the spring of 1770 all the Townshend Duties were removed, except the three pence per pound tax on tea. Following repeal, commerce between Britain and the colonies reached all-time highs. Relations between the colonists and mother country returned to normal, and for almost three years there were no serious disputes between them.

However, during this period of tranquility, the Radical Whigs were simply biding their time. They had come to the conclusion during the years of controversy that Parliament had no right to legislate for the colonies in any area whatsoever. The controversy had forced them to examine and analyze their society and their political ideals. It was clear to them that life in America was different than in England, and they quickly came to the conclusion that theirs was better. These men did not talk openly of independence, it was too dangerous and too early for that. But they waited for events to move their fellow Americans closer to independence, or for events to happen that they could manipulate.

In the spring of 1773, Parliament unwittingly gave the Whigs an issue. In 1773 the British East India Company was on the verge of bankruptcy. It could not pay its debts and its credit was almost exhausted. However, it was unthinkable to let this company collapse. If this company, the largest in the British Empire, fell, the resulting damage and chaos in the British economy would be devastating. This had to be prevented. Parliament knew that one of the reasons the East India Company was in distress was because the Americans had refused to buy British tea ever since it had been taxed by the Townshend Duties. They instead drank smuggled Dutch tea. For example New York's imports of English tea dropped from 320,000 pounds in 1768, to 530 pounds in 1772. Parliament decided to salvage the East India Company by helping it recapture the lucrative American market. By the Tea Act, 1773, Parliament assumed a closer supervisory role over the East India Company, and allowed it to ship tea directly to America. By eliminating the middleman, the company was able to sell tea in the colonies cheaper than in England itself, and was able to undersell the Dutch smugglers as well.

The Americans refused to be fooled by cheap tea. The tea was not only still taxed, but the East India Company had been given a virtual monopoly in selling tea in America. Many merchants feared that a monopoly in tea would be followed by a monopoly on selling wines, spices, and other imported commodities. Furthermore, a victory for the East India Company would be in reality a victory for the concept of Parliamentary taxation. The Whigs and Sons of Liberty everywhere in America organized to resist. Newspapers and pamphlets urged the public to stop drinking tea, and the women of America developed ingenious substitutes for the beverage. In many ports the Sons of Liberty prepared to prevent the landing of the taxed tea.

The most important such attempt was the Boston Tea Party. At Boston on the night of December 16, 1773, a band of men disguised as Indians, and led by Sam Adams and John Hancock, boarded the three tea ships and dumped 342 chests of tea, valued at over £15,000 into Boston Harbor, while several hundred townspeople cheered them on from the docks.

The reaction of Parliament to the Boston Tea Party was a determination to prevent this kind of defiance in the future and to punish Boston for wrong doing. Parliament was simply fed up with lawlessness in the colonies, and especially in Massachusetts. In the spring of 1774, Parliament enacted three measures, known as the Coercive Acts. First, the Port of Boston Act ordered the port closed to all shipping, except for food and firewood, until the people of Boston reimbursed the East India Company for the destroyed tea. Secondly, the Administration of Justice Act empowered the Governor to transfer to Britain for trial any official accused of a capital offense, if he was convinced that the official could not get a fair trial in Massachusetts. Thirdly, and most drastically, the Massachusetts Government Act altered the colony's charter which had been operative since 1691. The most important provisions of this Act were that henceforth the Council members were to be appointed by the Crown; sheriffs and justices of the peace were to be appointed by the Governor; juries were to be selected by the sheriffs, instead of being elected by the townspeople; and town meetings could only be held once a year, except with the prior written approval of the Governor, including his approval of the agenda of such meetings.

The passage of the Coercive Acts brought matters to a head. Boston could either yield to Parliamentary authority or it could continue to defy the mother country. To the Whig leaders, especially

Sam Adams, there was no turning back. They intended to resist, even if independence lay at the end of that road. As soon as news of the Port of Boston Act reached the city, the Boston Town Meeting, controlled by the Whigs, asked other towns and colonies to come to the city's aid. The Bostonians argued that Boston was the first line of defense for freedom in America. If Boston should fall, the power of Parliamentary tyranny would devour the other colonies "because the British government was making war upon liberty wherever it existed in the empire, and there could be no refuge in neutrality."

The reaction in the other colonies was instantaneous. Lord North's Coercive Acts had made the Bostonians martyrs in the eyes of most Americans. Towns from all parts of America responded by passing resolutions of support and by sending aid. One town denounced the British government as "instigated by the devil, and led on by the wicked and corrupt hearts of those pimps and parasites." The people of North Carolina believed, as did most Americans, that the "cause of Boston is the cause of all" and sent the ship *Penelope* containing 2,096 bushels of corn, 22 barrels of flour, and 17 barrels of pork to Massachusetts.

The need for inter-colonial cooperation in the face of the Coercive Acts was apparent to many. In the spring and early summer of 1774, many communities suggested that a general congress of the colonies be held. The Virginia House of Burgesses, meeting unofficially on May 27, sent a letter to all the colonies calling for such a meeting. The Massachusetts legislature, however, on June 17, named Philadelphia as the place, and September 1 as the time for the Continental Congress.

During the summer of 1774, in each colony, the Whigs were busy solidifying their support for action against Great Britain and deciding how to select delegates to the Continental Congress. In most colonies these delegates were chosen by the colonial assemblies, county conventions, or mass meetings of committees of correspondence. Only Georgia would be prevented from sending delegates by the opposition of her royal governor. In North Carolina, Governor Josiah Martin, who succeeded Governor Tryon in 1771, refused to summon the legislature into session for the purpose of selecting delegates to the Continental Congress. In response, Speaker of the House, John Harvey declared: "In that case the people will hold a convention independent of the Governor." On July 21, a convention of delegates from six counties met at Wilmington under the chairmanship of William Hooper. This group issued a call to all the counties in North Carolina to select delegates to attend a provincial meeting late in August at the Johnston County Court House in order to elect delegates to the Philadelphia meeting, as the best way to formulate and implement measures in concert with other colonies. A mass meeting in New Bern on August 9, however, urged the counties to send their delegates to New Bern, because the capital city was the most fitting place to hold the provincial meeting. The men most active in shifting the site for the provincial meeting were James Davis, Abner Nash, Isaac Taylor, Joseph Leech, Richard Cogdell, Richard Ellis, James Coor, David Barron and John Green.

During early August, the people of North Carolina defied Governor Martin, who was the highest representative of Royal authority in the colony, and proceeded to select delegates to the New Bern meeting. Seventy-one delegates from thirty of the thirty-six counties and six of the nine borough towns assembled as the First Provincial Congress on August 25, 1774. (This meeting should be called the First Provincial Convention, since this was the term used most frequently by contemporaries. However, "Congress" has been used by the state's most eminent historians, and has been sanctioned for many decades by the North Carolina Division of Archives and History.) Although the meeting lasted only three days, "it fully launched North Carolina into the revolutionary movement."

The delegates, after prudently proclaiming their loyalty to King George III, enumerated their grievances against the "powers unwarrantably assumed by the Parliament." The resolutions declared that "it is the very essence of the British Constitution that no subject should be taxed but by his ... legal representatives ... Therefore any act of Parliament imposing a tax is illegal and unconstitutional, That our Provincial Assemblies ... solely and exclusively possess that right." The resolutions expressed the delegates' alliance with the people of Massachusetts, who had "distinguished themselves in a manly support of the rights of America in general and that the cause in which they suffer is the Cause of every honest American." The resolutions declared that the Coercive Acts were unconstitutional. The resolutions proclaimed North Carolina's intention not to import any British goods, including slaves; not to consume any British goods already in the colony; and not to export any commodity to Great Britain. This aspect of North Carolina's defiance went further than any other colony's action by threatening to impose a similar boycott against any other province, town, or individual who failed to abide by the economic sanctions they expected to be adopted by the Continental Congress.

The resolutions endorsed the meeting of the Continental Congress in Philadelphia, and the delegates elected William Hooper, Joseph Hewes, and Richard Caswell as deputies to represent North Carolina. They were authorized to join with the representatives of other colonies in "a firm and resolute defence of our persons and properties against all unconstitutional encroachments whatever."

The first Provincial Congress was a very significant event in the early independence movement. It was the first elected assembly in America to be called and held in defiance of royal authority. It established the first revolutionary government in North Carolina in three ways. First, it required each county to contribute £20 proclamation money for the expenses of the delegates sent to Philadelphia. Secondly, it created the machinery of a new government by urging each county to select a committee of five persons to police the enforcement of the economic boycott just adopted. Thirdly, John Harvey was authorized to convene the delegates from the counties whenever he deemed it necessary without regard to "legal" formalities such as royal writs of election. Finally, the very process of electing delegates outside of the legal system gave a "practical demonstration of self-government, originating in the people."

Independence was still almost two years away when the First Provincial Congress adjourned on August 27, 1774. However, the Americans in the summer of 1774 had concluded that only their own elected assemblies, not Parliament, could pass laws for them. From this position the Americans refused to withdraw. Parliament, the Crown, and the Cabinet of Great Britain refused to accept this concept. There was no room for compromise. For two years, the Americans studiously refused to use the word "independence." Independence was a very dangerous and frightening prospect in the eighteenth century. For two years, every avenue of compromise and accommodation would be pursued, even after the armies started fighting. But neither side would give in. Not until January, 1776, when Tom Paine published *Common Sense*, did anyone in America call for independence in writing. Then after a decade of arguing over the basic rights of Englishmen, and months and months of trying to reach a compromise, were enough people finally convinced that declaring independence was the only alternative open to them. At last, a great new nation would be born.

Post Office Building

Christ Episcopal Church

# WEATHER VANES

Weather vanes have gone out of style in recent years, but several buildings in New Bern have managed to retain these quaint relics of the past.

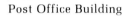

First Presbyterian Church

County Court House

# THE ARCHITECTURE OF NEW BERN

**By Janet K. Seapker, Survey Specialist
Survey and Planning Unit, Division of
Archives and History, Department of
Cultural Resources**

Architecture is a three-dimensional testimony of the history of an area or town—a testimony to its growth and development pattern, its commercial and cultural contacts, its receptiveness to change and to current vogues, its political and religious biases, and its eras and levels of prosperity; so it is with the architecture of New Bern.

The architecture of New Bern testifies to the history of a coastal town whose commercial orientation was external, a town which has been subject to and receptive to major architectural trends, and one which for the most part has enjoyed sustained prosperity. Each of North Carolina's coastal towns has its own individual architectural identity. New Bern's architecture is academic, rendered in a sedate, restrained manner—quite unlike the bold, flamboyant interpretation popular in Wilmington or the functional vernacular styles expressed in Beaufort's cottages.

New Bern is thought of as a primarily colonial town, and indeed, by the Revolution, it had become a substantial port and an important political center with a concentration of handsome Georgian buildings, a few of which remain. Yet it was in the Federal era (post-Revolutionary period) that New Bern underwent a dramatic architectural efflorescence that produced a body of urban Federal style structures of academic sophistication and superb craftsmanship seldom rivaled in the country. The Federal style had a remarkably tenacious hold on New Bern, lasting until the late 1840s—some twenty years after it had been superseded by the Greek Revival style in most coastal areas of the country. There are virtually no Greek Revival style buildings in New Bern, for by the time the town relinquished the Federal style and rejoined the national architectural mainstream, mid-nineteenth century eclecticism was the fashion. Residential, public, and commercial structures, built in a variety of Victorian styles ranging from Italianate and Renaissance Revival styles to the later Queen Anne and Stick styles are still very much in evidence. The last period of major economic growth in the downtown area coincided with the popularity of the Neo-Classical Revival style, and thus that style too is well represented.

New Bern is set on a triangular land area defined by the Trent and Neuse Rivers. The rivers once bustled with mercantile and fishing ships, but now they form a serene backdrop for the town's sophisticated buildings. Most of New Bern's streets are quiet ones, punctuated by buildings set on large, well-landscaped lots, and shaded by stately trees whose branches are dotted with clumps of mistletoe.

The relatively high survival rate of New Bern's old structures is complemented by the survival of the original town plan and the quality of spaciousness. When the city was established in 1710, Baron von Graffenried requested John Lawson to devise and lay out the town plan, which with some additions, remains intact. Lawson explained:

> Since in America they do not like to live crowded, in order to enjoy a purer air, I accordingly ordered the streets to be very broad and the houses well separated one from the other. I marked three acres of land for each family, for house, barn, garden, orchard, hemp field, poultry yard and other purposes. I divided the village like a cross and in the middle I intended a church. One of the principal streets extended from the bank of the River Neuse straight on into the forest (Broad or Pollock Street) and the principal street crossed it, running from the Trent River clear to the Neuse River (Middle or Craven Street). After that we planted stakes to mark the houses and to make the principal streets along and on the banks of the two rivers [East Front Street and South Front Street (now Tryon Palace Drive)].

Not only has the street scheme survived, but also the idea of not liking to "live crowded" is still in evidence. With the exception of the construction accomplished since the mid-twentieth century and four mid-nineteenth century row houses, all residences are separate, free-standing buildings, each with a generous yard—quite a different situation from the row houses tightly packed together in the more northern coastal cities of Baltimore, Georgetown, Annapolis, Philadelphia, Boston, etc.

Historically, New Bern has been dependent for its livelihood on its rivers and on governmental sponsorship. The city's role as occasional host of the itinerant colonial assembly, the colony's first permanent capital, and the seat of Craven County helped foster her emergence as a port and therefore as a mercantile center. Shortly before the Revolution, Governor Josiah Martin observed,

It is true ... the Town of Beaufort, is advantageously situated for commerce, but there are no persons of condition or substance in it, and the Trade what was formerly carried on through that channel, is now derived almost entirely to this Town [New Bern], since it became the seat of government, which has promoted its growth exceedingly, by inviting many considerable Merchants to settle in it.

This external orientation of the town's economy brought the residents into contact with the major ports of this country, England, and the West Indies, and gave them access to constantly changing life styles and architectural modes. The effect of this contact on the architecture of the town is obvious, for the vast majority of structures express a high degree of academicism successfully rendered by skilled and sensitive craftsmen.

### The Georgian Style in New Bern (Eighteenth Century)

Nothing remains of the earliest buildings. Even a comparison of New Bern today with what C. J. Sauthier recorded on his 1769 map of the town finds only four buildings which tentatively are identified as surviving from that time. (Not included in this figure is the Governor's Palace, most of which burned in 1798 and was reconstructed in the 1950s).

Fifteen Georgian-style buildings, most dating from the last quarter of the eighteenth century, have been identified in New Bern. This is a scant number considering that more than thirty house carpenters and/or joiners are known to have been working in the county between 1748 and 1790. With the exception of a few houses attributed either to John Hawks or to James Coor, the architect-builder of most buildings cannot be identified. It can be assumed that natural attrition combined with disasters like the hurricane of September, 1769, and the fires in the fall of 1791 and 1794, and that of February, 1798, which burned the Governor's Palace, eradicated much of the evidence of the early town.

A study of the fifteen remaining Georgian style buildings does not reveal any typical type or form. About the only feature common to all is a heavy timber frame covered with weatherboards; size, roof forms, plans, and chimney placement vary greatly. While the gable roof (both with and without dormers) is the most common form, four of the Georgian style dwellings have gambrel roofs.

Two of the buildings are set on foundations of coquina, a shell-rock conglomerate native to the New Bern area.

Because of the variety of exterior forms used in Georgian style buildings, the style is most easily recognized from viewing the interior finish. Commonly found Georgian features include doors composed of six raised panels; mantels with a molded architrave surrounding the fire opening, a flush frieze with console endblocks supporting a heavily molded cornice shelf; some form of wainscot with molded chair rail and baseboard; closed or openstring stair with turned or square-section balusters supporting a heavily molded handrail. The ornamentation of these features varies considerably accordingly to the elaborateness of the structure. Designs for these features and instructions for making them were contained in pattern books or builders' guides. Although the instructions and designs allowed room for the builder to make his own interpretation, the New Bern house carpenter seemed to follow closely the book when finishing the interiors of a Georgian style house.

While only fifteen Georgian style structures have survived, a description of New Bern in 1787 written by William Attmore provides more clues as to what the town's buildings must have looked like.

There are [,] to many of the houses [,] Balconies or Piazzas in front and sometimes back of the house, this Method of Building is found convenient on account of the great Summer Heats here—These Balconies are often two Stories high, sometimes one or both ends of it [them] are boarded up, and made in to a Room.

The Coor-Gaston House (see p. 44) best represents the type of structure Attmore described. The two-tier porch enclosed by a balustrade in the Chinese Chippendale motif, is such an integral part of the living area of the house that it is finished in the manner of an interior—complete with flush-sheathed walls and molded cornice, chair rail, and baseboard.

The end of the Georgian style of architecture followed on the heels of the end of British rule over the colonies. By that time, the Georgian style, the British version of Baroque architecture, was on the wane in England as well. Although the Revolution brought political separation between the American colonies and England, strong cultural and commercial ties continued to exist. For many years to follow, America took cues from her former mother country, while altering and interpreting them in her own milieu.

## The Federal Style in New Bern (ca. 1790-1840)

Within the last two decades of the eighteenth century the population of New Bern more than doubled, and the physical area of the town accordingly expanded north and west; this trend continued in the first decades of the nineteenth century. Obviously the town was enjoying a new high level of prosperity—a prosperity based on commercial and mercantile endeavors which enabled affluent merchants like John Harvey, Eli Smallwood, and Isaac Taylor to build ambitious town houses. It was during this same era of prosperity that the town produced civic and cultural symbols of urbanization, most notably the New Bern Academy (see p. 62), the Masonic Temple and Theater (see p. 60), and the First Presbyterian Church (see p. 92).

The prosperity of early nineteenth century New Bern coincided with the emergence of the Federal style. Originating in England, the style was essentially that of the brothers Adam who designed interiors in a delicate light manner, employing classical details and forms which had been recorded by archaeologists investigating the ruins of the ancient Roman cities. The Adam, or as it is known in America, Federal style, gained popularity coincidentally with the separation of the colonies from British rule and thus was partially a cultural response to an ideological-political trend. In themselves the classical elements employed in the Federal style symbolize the republican ideals subscribed to by the ancient Roman civilization. As royal rule gave way to the Federal Constitution, so the robust English Georgian style was superseded by the delicate Federal style, the first truly American architectural statement. Be it for ideological reasons or purely aesthetic ones, New Bern excelled in the Federal style.

While no one form of Georgian architecture predominated in New Bern, a very specific type and form of Federal architecture can be identified; it is Adamesque, that is, academic and very much according to the book. Federal style architecture in New Bern is restrained, elegant, and above all, sophisticated. It employs delicate elements ornamented with intricate carved and gouged motifs; to be appreciated properly, it must be studied at close range.

A typical New Bern Federal domestic structure has the following elements: two-and-one-half stories; a side-hall plan, two rooms deep (three bays wide and four bays deep); a gable roof; gable dormer windows; exposed-face chimneys; a one-bay pedimented porch; an entrance composed of a six-panel door (four flat above two flush panels) with geometrically ornamented transom above. Interior Federal features include a transverse arch in the hall; open-string stair with balusters and newel square-in-section, the newel and secondary posts being tapered; a rounded handrail which ramps and eases over the newel and posts; and wave pattern stair brackets. Mantels on the first two floors are invariably three-part mantels following Adamesque lines. These mantels have pilasters flanking the fire opening and carrying a classically derived entablature composed of an architrave, frieze and molded cornice. The frieze usually breaks out to form end blocks and a center tablet, and the cornice serves as the mantel shelf. Doors and windows are cased in molded architraves consisting of three parts. Doors are of six panels with all panels being flat. (These doors are referred to properly as six-panel doors, not "cross and Bible doors".)

Because so much of the Federal style is contained in the intricate ornament, it is only fitting to discuss the types and patterns used. The sunburst and fan motifs occur almost exclusively on center tablets and end blocks of mantels. Bands of guilloche occur in chair rails of the more elaborate buildings. In the ornamental transoms, the wooded members which hold the pieces of glass in place are augmented by carved festoons, garlands, goddesses, rosettes, and/or sunbursts. The greatest variety of ornament occurs on cornices—both exterior and interior. Modillions, dentil courses of all varieties, cable moldings, scallop bands, etc. are juxtaposed in almost endless combinations. Builders' manuals of the time illustrated in detail all of these patterns and quite obviously were the source of the ornament. A local tradition holds that the profuse use of the cable molding is explained by the fact that the houses were executed by ships carpenters. There is no documentation to support such a contention. Carpenters of the eighteenth and nineteenth centuries who recorded their apprentices in the county records were very specific as to the nature of their carpentry—house carpenter or shipwright. With these facts in mind there can be no doubt that the cable molding was a product of the builders' guides and not a localized derivation from the ropes used on the wharves and ships of New Bern.

All the side-hall plan Federal houses have been altered in some manner to adapt them for modern living: extensions built in a style contemporary to the time of the addition provide needed space for expanding families; electricity and plumbing have been installed. The alterations in many cases are not disturbing and actually enhance the architectural value of the building by providing a stylistic and utilitarian bridge. For the most part, the alterations have extended the life of the buildings, keeping them up-to-date for modern life.

Of the twenty-four typical New Bern side-hall plan Federal style buildings, seven are constructed of brick and the remainder of wooden frame covered with weatherboards. One of the twenty-four has a gambrel roof and two others can be considered one-and-one-half story cottages. While alterations and additions may have obscured the original side-hall form of some of this group of houses, all started out with that configuration. Although the side-hall plan was certainly the most prevalent Federal form, center-hall and asymmetrical versions were built as well. A concentration of those which survive occurs on Pollock Street in the area west of Tryon Palace, but others are scattered throughout the town. Usually they are two or two-and-one-half story frame structures (three are of brick) with gable roofs (two have gambrel roofs), exposed-face chimneys, and Federal interior woodwork. These structures range from quite modest to very elaborate, with the woodwork varying accordingly.

Three public buildings have survived from the early Federal period—the New Bern Academy (1806), the Masonic Temple and Theater (1801-1809), and the First Presbyterian Church (1819-1822). The Academy (see p. 62), perhaps the design of William Nichols who worked later in Edenton, Raleigh, Chapel Hill, and Hillsborough, has survived remarkably for having been in continuous use until 1972. The fanlight, the cornice of coupled modillions and the semi-circular entrance porch are very much like Nichols' work on Hayes Plantation. The Masonic Temple and Theater (see p. 60), although the exterior has been greatly expanded and altered, contains a well-preserved lodge room at the second level. The elaborate woodwork, the work of John Dewey, is juxtaposed with Masonic symbols painted in the *trompe l'oeil* manner on the walls about 1847 by an unknown itinerant artist. The masterpiece of the Federal style civic buildings is the First Presbyterian Church (see p. 92). It is the work of a local architect builder, Uriah Sandy, who in 1804 at the age of fourteen was apprenticed to New Bern house carpenter Benjamin Good. This dispels the notion that Sandy was a Connecticut architect who migrated south and built the church in the style popular in New England at the time. Even if Sandy was a Connecticut native, his architectural training was local. And as with the cable molding, the design of the church is quite like those which appear in the builders' guides, one or more of which he probably owned. The structure is most notable for its perfect symmetry outside and inside. Particularly pleasing is the foyer which is balanced at each end by a transverse arch framing a graceful spiraling stair. The barrel-vaulted sanctuary, lined with galleries carried on slender columns, has as its focal point a raised pulpit which was meticulously restored in 1936. Although this towered church is very different from other churches of the era, several features typical of New Bern link the First Presbyterian Church to other buildings in town—the sanctuary cornice with its cable molding and delicate modillions, the balustrades of the foyer stairs and those flanking the pulpit, the traditional system of flat and flush panels used on the exterior doors, and the delicate fanlights. The construction of the church is well-documented in the account books of William Hollister, a merchant who supplied the building materials to Sandy.

In the Federal era the authorship of several buildings can be attributed with varying degrees of certainty to Martin Stevenson, John Dewey, Robert Hay, William Nichols, and Uriah Sandy—five of some forty architect-builders working in the county between 1790 and 1835. As in the Georgian era, this leaves the majority of structures for which no designer can be determined.

The Federal style persisted in New Bern well into the 1840s, long after it had been superseded by the Greek Revival style in other towns. This was by no means a result of cultural lag; rather it would seem more likely to be a product of conservative mercantile interests, a proposition set forth by Talbot Hamlin in *Greek Revival Architecture in America:*

> There were great mercantile and shipping interests, particularly of Boston and Philadelphia, for whom England and the English colonists were still the best—and almost the only—customers. Artistic conservatism often persisted, owing to the fact that many of the skilled craftsmen of the country were either English-trained or but one generation removed from England, and to the fact that, in architecture at least, all of them depended largely on English books.

The importance of such mercantile interests in New Bern, combined with the habits of the craftsmen, provide a cogent explanation for the longevity of the Federal style in the city.

## The Greek Revival Style in New Bern (ca. 1830-1850)

So tenaciously did the town cling to Federal architecture that it scarcely acknowledged the existence of other styles. Concessions to the Greek Revival style usually appear on the interiors of buildings and most often take the form of symmetrically molded architraves with corner blocks. In the houses which exhibit Greek Revival tendencies, the standard flat broad Greek Revival molding supersedes the delicate Federal moldings on six panel doors. In the more elaborate houses, marble mantels were ordered for the main parlors, and in the more modest houses, simple Federal style mantels remained the norm. Although one would expect to find a heavy stair treatment (bulbous turned newel post, turned balusters, and a broad molded handrail) in buildings of the Greek Revival era, those in New Bern exhibit the same delicate stair of the Federal style buildings. In only a very few cases are classical Greek motifs employed externally, the most obvious example being the pure Greek Doric porch on the Attmore-Oliver House (see p. 61), added when other alterations were made to the dwelling in the 1830s. The popular image of the great columned antebellum mansion of the South, has no representative in New Bern, nor from what documentary photographs show, did it ever. The Greek Revival style in New Bern is not expressed in a full-blown classical temple, but rather as transitional; the buildings display the full range of application of Greek Revival motifs in and on basically Federal forms. While other good examples of this transitional approach to the Greek Revival style exist, the most striking is the William Hollister House (see p. 69), built in 1840-1841, which from the street looks like the standard side-hall Federal style dwelling. It is only at close observation that the flat broad moldings on the six-panel door are seen. Inside, the same treatment occurs—with Greek Revival moldings being used on woodwork of Federal design.

## Mid-Nineteenth Century Eclecticism in New Bern (ca. 1840-1855)

By the time New Bern rejoined the mainstream of national architectural trends, the Greek Revival style was waning, and mid-nineteenth century eclecticism was flourishing. The town began to experiment with the new styles in the 1840s. The incidence of buildings constructed in the pre-Civil War eclectic era is lower than that of earlier eras. Probably in part this is due to the leveling-off of both the population and wealth of New Bern.

Although others existed, only one early Italianate dwelling survives, that being the Thomas Jerkins House (see p. 80). Here, brackets, the hallmark of the Italianate style, support overhanging eaves of the low pitched roof, which rests on what is essentially a traditional New Bern side-hall dwelling.

The Edward R. Stanly House and Dependency (see p. 81), and the Slover-Bradham House (see p. 76) are New Bern's two solid representatives of the Renaissance Revival style. This is an urban mode characterized by strictly contained rectangular blocks—not interrupted by projections of any sort. The entrance level is elevated above the basement, and occasionally accentuated by a balcony as in the Slover-Bradham House. It is common for the window size to diminish at each floor level. The stately massiveness of the Slover-Bradham House is unrivaled in New Bern and in the state; indeed it would fit quite comfortably amid the town houses on Beacon Hill in Boston.

During this era the congregation of the First Baptist Church (see p. 94) elected to build a new edifice and obtained a Gothic Revival design from the New York firm of Thomas and Son. Universally recognized by the pointed arch, the Gothic Revival style is most commonly associated with church architecture. Indeed First Baptist Church displays other characteristics of the Gothic Revival style, specifically in the crenelated battlements which crown the tower and in the doors carved with Gothic motifs.

New Bern retained a degree of independence of design and materials during the era of participation in the national eclectic mainstream. This is best demonstrated in the wall and arched gateway of Cedar Grove Cemetery (see p. 101) constructed of native coquina by the town in 1854.

## Post Civil War Eclecticism in New Bern (ca. 1870-1900)

The decades following the Civil War are related to the ones preceding it in that there were numerous architectural styles were popular at the same time, but, there is a difference. Rather than repeating or imitating ancient styles, the postwar modes were completely new which, for the most part, took cues from nature and were constructed of new materials and building components produced by machines. Some of the later eclectic styles and their representatives in New Bern are: Second Empire—Stimson House (see p. 74); late Italianate Revival—Judge Manly House (see p. 75); Romanesque Revival—New Bern Municipal Building (see p. 90); Queen Anne—George Slover House (see p. 84); Stick Style—All Saints' Chapel (see p. 104); Carpenter Gothic—barn (218 Metcalf Street, see p. 82). Christ Church (see p. 93) rebuilt between 1871 and 1875 in the late Gothic Revival style, is enhanced by the handsome Stick-style porch added in 1887. Since eclecticism is the nature of the post Civil War era, many buildings, especially commercial structures like the Albert Hotel (see p. 106), and the Shoemasters Store (see p. 106), cannot be categorized in any specific style, but are simply Victorian. While each postwar style has features which separate it apart from others, there are basic characteristics which are held in common. The buildings are not confined to strict rectangular lines, but are asymmetrical, frequently interrupted by projections like bay windows or towers; floor plans are irregular, so that one can not determine the interior plan simply from viewing the exterior. This freedom of design is in part due to the use of the balloon frame—the light type of frame used in construction today. The earlier timber framing method employed huge sills, beams and plates which were held together by pegged mortise and tenon joints. While timber framing is incredibly strong and durable, it doesn't allow for freedom of design. A rectangle or square was about all the choice allotted. Machine-made ornament in the form of sawn brackets, patterned shingles, finials, molded window cornices, etc., add a variety of texture to the exterior surface. A substantial portion of the late nineteenth century domestic structures, especially the more massive ones, have met with destruction, but a few of them, plus a number of smaller, more manageable houses survive.

### Neo-Classical Revival Style in New Bern (ca. 1900-1910)

In the early twentieth century New Bern experienced a building boom which in volume came close to rivaling the Federal boom. The economic revitalization of the town was largely a result of the lumber industry which produced magnates desirous of living in and capable of paying for the most impressive houses their money could buy. Obliging these clients was a local architect, Herbert Woodley Simpson, who is credited with the design of almost every important structure built in New Bern in the first decade of the twentieth century. A versatile designer, Simpson excelled in the Queen Anne and Neo-Classical Revival styles and often combined the two as he did in his tour de force, the W. B. Blades House (see p. 85). The colossal order classical porticos on the L. I. Moore House (see p. 87), and on the now demolished J. B. Blades House (Queen Anne Hotel) best expressed the classical idiom of Simpson's domestic work. Two ecclesiastical structures, the First Church of Christ, Scientist (see p. 97), and Temple B'nai Sholem (see p. 99), both pedimented temple-form structures, are beautifully rendered expressions of the Neo-Classical Revival style. The Elks Temple (see p. 105), constructed by Rhoads and Underwood of Wilmington, and the former First Citizens Bank (see p. 105), designed by Burett Stephens of Wilmington are two examples of the use of the classical style in commercial structures.

After the first decade of the twentieth century, the development of suburban communities decreased residential construction within the city. The advent of World War II brought in swarms of armed service personnel attached to nearby Cherry Point Air Base. To accommodate the considerable overflow from Cherry Point, New Bernians opened their homes and divided other stately houses into apartments. Some of the alterations were sympathetically done, but in other cases buildings were mutilated.

In the 1940s Minnette (Mrs. Richard) Duffy inspired and initiated the movement to reconstruct the governor's palace. Mrs. Maude Moore Latham established two trust funds for the reconstruction. The actual construction, which began in the mid-1950s, necessitated the closing of George Street. Known as the Tryon Palace complex, the area includes the reconstructed palace; the Stevenson House (see p. 35), a restored Federal era house museum; the Daves House (see p. 34), used for administrative offices; the Jones House (see p. 34), a guest house; and the John Wright Stanly House (see p. 36), a Georgian style house museum. The development of the historical complex has been instrumental in bringing visitors into New Bern.

The commercial district was well established along lower Middle Street, Pollock Street and Tryon Palace Drive (then South Front Street). It remained fairly constant except for facade modernizations until the 1950s when Broad Street was designated U. S. 70. That designation ruined the residential nature of Broad Street—trees were cut down, house after house was bulldozed to make room for gasoline stations, quick food outlets, and parking lots. Broad Street, still a major east-west thoroughfare, cleaves the old city into two pieces.

If New Bern is to retain the architectural character with which the residents of preceding centuries endowed her, her present residents must exercise constant vigilance against unsympathetic landowners and developers. New Bern's streetscape, that is, the concentration of architecturally significant buildings which one sees from the street, is one of her most important resources. Each building bears a vital visual relationship to its neighbors. When these relationships are eliminated through demolition, a snaggletooth effect is created—an effect attractive to neither resident nor visitor. Architectural preservation has been proven to be economically feasible and profitable in city after city. New Bern has an abundance of architectural resources—her only task now is to realize the potential and act on it.

# THE TRYON PALACE RESTORATION COMPLEX

**By Donald Ransone Taylor**

The center of the Tryon Palace Complex is Tryon Palace, with its main building and the two wings containing the Kitchen and Stables. Moved within the Complex in 1966, the John Wright Stanly House is an elegant New Bern home of the 1780's, the home of the prominent businessman and Revolutionary War patriot, John Wright Stanly. Here President George Washington spent two nights in April, 1791 while on his Southern tour. He recorded in his diary that these were "exceeding good lodgings." The Stevenson House, built upon one of the original Palace lots around 1805, features furnishings of the Federal era. Administrative offices are housed in the ca. 1810 McKinlay-Daves home. Here Mary McKinlay Daves married Governor John Willis Ellis in 1858. The Jones House, built in 1808-1809, serves as the guest house of the Tryon Palace Commission.

In 1764 William Tryon was chosen by England's King George III to serve as lieutenant governor of the Royal Colony of North Carolina, under Governor Arthur Dobbs. Tryon first went to Brunswick, where Dobbs maintained his residence and where the colonial legislature frequently met. In March, 1765, Governor Dobbs died and William Tryon assumed the office of Royal Governor.

It was due largely to Tryon's efforts that New Bern was selected as the colonial capital. Tryon had brought with him from England an architect, John Hawks, who was commissioned to design and supervise the construction of the government house. The colonial legislature appropriated £15,000 for the construction. Hawks obtained some craftsmen from Philadelphia to work on the project. Construction was begun in 1767, and Governor Tryon, Mrs. Tryon and their nine year old daughter, Margaret, moved into Tryon's Palace in June, 1770. Many westerners, objecting to being taxed and never expecting to see the building, referred to the government house as "Tryon's Palace."

Tryon Palace served as both the official government building of the colony and the residence of the governor and his family. While a number of rooms on the first floor served its official government function, there are rooms on the second floor for the private use of the family. Tryon Palace was designed by an English architect for an English royal governor who furnished it with his own English furniture.

Before the Battle of Alamance, during which Tryon led colonial militiamen in the defeat of the Regulators, Tryon received orders from King George III to report to the Colony of New York to serve as Royal Governor. He was replacing John Murray, Earl of Dunmore who was sent to govern Virginia. On June 30, 1771, Governor Tryon, with his wife and daughter and personal belongings embarked for Fort George, New York.

Tryon's successor at New Bern was Josiah Martin, who arrived on August 11, 1771. Impressed with the Palace which Tryon had built, Martin contracted with John Hawks to build a smokehouse, dovecote, and poultry house on the grounds, and to enclosed the Palace Square with a fence.

Royal Governor Josiah Martin was received respectfully by the New Bernians upon his arrival and governed well for his first two years in office. But Martin was soon caught up in the times and any representative of British authority would have difficulty governing.

Upon the departure of Josiah Martin from New Bern in May, 1775, Tryon Palace gradually emerged as the capitol of the newly-formed state of North Carolina. Its first legislative assembly met there in April, 1776. Tryon Palace was the site of the inaugurations of four early state governors and a frequent site of legislative meetings. In 1794 the new capital was established at Raleigh and four years later, in 1798, the main building of Tryon Palace was destroyed by fire. Commissioners appointed by the General Assembly in 1799 sold the Palace lots, and streets, lots, houses and other buildings replaced the grandeur of Tryon Palace. Its East Wing disappeared during the nineteenth century, and only its West Wing remained to welcome its restoration.

Many people dreamed for years of the re-

**Tryon Palace.**

The Governor's Bedroom is beautifully furnished with an English bed approximately six feet wide and six feet long, Massachusetts highboy and English Wilton carpet. The brass chandelier was found on the island of Barbadoes.

In the Parlor of Tryon Palace stands a figure wearing the dress of Mrs. Eunice Kelly of New Bern. Mrs. Kelly wore this dress to the ball given at Tryon Palace for President George Washington during his 1791 Southern Tour.

In the Council Chamber, the large portraits of King George III and his Queen, Charlotte, were constant reminders to the governor and council of the source of their authority. The inventory of furnishings of Royal Governor William Tryon listed portraits of England's rulers.

construction of Tryon Palace. Even the proceeds of the 1929 historical pageant were earmarked for this project. School children contributed their pennies as Mrs. Richard N. Duffy of New Bern worked with other New Bernians towards their ultimate goal of restoration of Tryon Palace. John Hawks' original plans for the Palace were found in New York in 1939 but World War II dashed any hopes of initiation of the project at that time. It was a native New Bernian, then a resident of Greensboro, Mrs. Maude Moore Latham, who established two trust funds in the late 1940's for the restoration of Tryon Palace. In 1945, largely through the efforts of the late Mr. D. L. Ward, member of the State Senate, the State of North Carolina made its first appropriation of funds for Tryon Palace. In October, 1945, Governor Gregg Cherry appointed the first members of the Tryon Palace Commission, with Mrs. Latham as Chairman. In July, 1950, the first five tracts of land of the original site were purchased by the State of North Carolina.

Reconstruction of Tryon Palace began in 1952. The West Wing, the one original building, was converted from a stucco-covered apartment house to the Palace stables once again. Guided by Governor Tryon's inventory of furnishings, members of the Commission's Acquisitions Committee purchased much of the furniture for the restored Palace in England and Scotland in 1957. The gardens were designed in the eighteenth century English manner and the on-going process of planting began. On April 8, 1959 Tryon Palace was officially opened to the public.

Since its opening, hundreds of thousands of visitors have come to see and hear the history of Tryon Palace, New Bern, and North Carolina. In this authentic setting, living history can be truly taught. The Palace affords an appropriate backdrop for the history of the Royal Colony of North Carolina, 1765-1776, and of the struggling new and independent state, 1776-1798. Here history was made and here history can be retold to make North Carolinians and all Americans more appreciative of their rich heritage. Here we can trod the paths of the patriots of yesteryear; here we can pay tribute to their inestimable contributions to our way of life today.

**McKinlay-Daves House:** (613 Pollock Street). Adaptively restored as administrative offices for the Tryon Palace Restoration staff.

**Jones House:** (231 Eden Street). Guest House of the Tryon Palace Commission noted for its beautiful southern style garden.

**Stevenson House:** (609 Pollock Street) Built ca. 1805 on one of the original Palace lots, it is an important addition to the Restoration Complex, affording the opportunity to display furniture of the Federal Era.

The two drawing rooms are expressions of elegant living in the early nineteenth century. In the front drawing room one can see an English Sheraton fancy chair, Philadelphia sofa and South Carolina Pembroke table. The carpet is an Herez and the chandelier is English, ca. 1820.

The Stevenson House is highly regarded because of its fine, original, hand-carved woodwork, and its spacious hallway featuring an arch with a carved keystone and rope or cable molding.

The Tulip Bedroom, with its French wallpaper, contains a New England maple field bed, corner washstand and small Hepplewhite tables. The pillar and scroll mantel clock was made by Eli Terry.

35

**John Wright Stanly House:** (307 George Street). Built in the 1780s, the Stanly House was moved to the Tryon Palace Complex in 1966 and opened in 1972. The home of John Wright Stanly, patriot of the Revolution, shipowner, and businessman. General Ambrose Burnside used it as his first New Bern headquarters during the Civil War. The City of New Bern wisely saved this famous residence and gave it to the Tryon Palace Commission after having used it as a library.

B

A. The parterre garden of the Stanly House has a stone wellhead as its focal point. In the background the gazebos can be seen.

B. The Massachusetts secretary and Philadelphia chairs in the Stanly House Drawing Room reflect New Bern's coastwise trade and Stanly's Philadelphia business associations. Most of the paneling is original; the chandelier is Waterford and the carpet is an Axminster.

C. The most elaborate of the Stanly bedrooms could have been the one occupied for two nights in April, 1791 by President George Washington. No records exist which tell us which room he used.

C

A

**Maude Moore Latham Memorial Garden.** This Garden, with its memorial pavilion, honors the restoration donor. The garden is of the English landscape design, a type with which Governor Tryon would have been familiar in England. Tulips and violas bloom each spring, followed by a variety of plants blooming throughout the summer and chrysanthemums each fall.

**Kellenberger Garden.** Honoring Mr. and Mrs. John A. Kellenberger, the late Treasurer and present Chairman of the Tryon Palace Commission, the small, walled Garden is a privy garden, designed for viewing from within the building by members of the household.

**Green Garden.** All of the plant material within this garden, with the exception of the blooms of the Crepe Myrtle, is green. The statue in the center of the garden was brought from Mrs. Latham's Greensboro garden. This is also a privy garden.

# GEORGIAN STYLE HOUSES

**Clear Springs Plantation:** (rural Craven County). Also known as Green's Thoroughfare or the Dawson Place, this Georgian frame house is the earliest standing structure in the county, possibly built as early as 1740. An unusual amount of fine woodwork has survived, including beaded baseboards, molded chair rail, and a deep molded cornice. Almost all interior doors retain their original HL hinges. The land was granted to Farnifold Green in 1707 and settled before the arrival of de Graffenried. The property has been in the possession of the Dawson family since 1707.

Note the "marl" foundation. This is the earliest known use of coquina, a shell-rock conglomerate native to the area, for a foundation. The outcropping of marl on the Plantation would later be used in most of the houses in New Bern and on the Cedar Grove Cemetery wall.

**Hawks House:** (306 Hancock Street). Southern part of house was built ca. 1760 in Georgian style; northern expansion added between 1780 and 1820 is finished in Federal style. All rooms have plaster walls, molded chair rails and baseboards, and simple Adamesque mantels. Doors carry early HL hinges and carpenter locks. Purchased in 1807 by Francis Hawks, son of John Hawks, the architect of Tryon Palace. Francis served as Collector of Customs in New Bern for thirty-two years. His son, Francis Lister Hawks, became a noted Episcopal Bishop and historian.

**Major James Daves House:** (313 George Street). Georgian style coastal cottage was built in the late eighteenth century; home of famous Revolutionary patriot. House has been adaptively restored by Mr. and Mrs. P. C. Dorsey.

**Bellair Plantation:** (.3 mile north from junction of SR-1401 and SR-1419 in rural Craven County). Property was first taken up by John Swift before 1719. Building was built in stages: the exterior by the Spaight family in the 1760s; the interior, east wing, by the Wilson Blounts in the 1780s; and the interior, west wing, by Thomas Kean in the early 1800s. Purchased in 1838 by John H. Richardson, whose descendants still own it. Bellair received special protection from Gen. Burnside during the Civil War Occupation. Residence of Mr. and Mrs. G. Tull Richardson.

Front door is a massive eight panel door which still contains the original lock box with fine pendant handles.

Mantel in dining room.

Kitchen with early utensils.

Bellair's closed-string stair.

Georgian stair is so similar to that in the John Wright Stanly House as to indicate that the house was designed by John Hawks.

Detail of elegant transverse arch in the entrance hall.

**Coor-Bishop House:** (501 East Front Street). Georgian style house built ca. 1767 by James Coor and remodeled in early twentieth century by Herbert W. Simpson in Neo-Classical Revival style during the ownership of Edward K. Bishop. Coor was active in Revolutionary and early national politics, and worked with John Hawks on the construction of Tryon Palace; later owned by George Pollock when, in 1819, President James Monroe and Sec. of War and Mrs. John C. Calhoun were entertained here. Residence of Dr. and Mrs. Raymond Houghton.

**Coor-Bishop House Dependency:** (214 New Street). A mid-nineteenth century structure, probably used for slave quarters. Residence of Mr. and Mrs. J. Gaskill McDaniel.

**Brinson House:** (213 Johnson Street). Built before the Revolution. First floor was remodeled in the Victorian period, but exterior and second floor Georgian woodwork remain. Residence of Mrs. Carl F. Bunting.

**Judge Gaston Law Office:** (307 Craven Street). Moved to present site in 1949. Restored and maintained by the New Bern Garden Club.

**House at 217 Hancock Street.** Residence of Mr. Roy C. Setzer.

**Elijah Clark House:** (616 Middle Street). Late eighteenth century frame house was owned by Elijah Clark who was Sheriff of Craven County, and one of the founders of First Baptist Church. House was saved by the Historic New Bern Foundation, and is being restored by Mr. and Mrs. William Smith.

**York-Gordon House:** (213 Hancock Street). This frame gambrel roof house was begun in the 1760s by Stephen York, and completed by Patrick Gordon in the 1770s. The residence has both Georgian and Federal elements, and the property originally ran to the Trent River. One of only two pre-Revolutionary gambrel roof houses surviving in New Bern. Residence of Mrs. Georgia W. Tosto.

**Mary Hatch Harrison House:** (219 New Street). Mrs. Harrison was instrumental in establishing the Christian Science Church in New Bern.

**Coor-Gaston House:** (421 Craven Street). This well preserved pre-Revolutionary (ca. 1770) Georgian house was built by the patriot James Coor. The house was purchased in 1818 by Judge William Gaston, a distinguished lawyer; member of Congress; justice of the State Supreme Court; composer of the state song, "The Old North State"; crusader for abolishment of religious qualifications for office holding; and an early outspoken opponent of slavery. Under Gaston's influence, the house was the site for the founding of St. Paul's Roman Catholic Church when Bishop John England of the Diocese of Charleston celebrated the first Mass in North Carolina here on May 24, 1821.

This frame house, with its two-tier porches with Chinese Chippendale balustrades, is unique in New Bern. Interior woodwork displays a variety of well-executed Georgian themes. The house is now being restored by the Judge Gaston House Restoration Association.

44

**Smith-Whitford House:** (506 Craven Street). This house demonstrates the unique combination of the very best elements from two periods: the Georgian and the Victorian. The house was built ca. 1772 for Henry Smith, and was probably designed by James Coor. Victorian alterations, including the entrance, side porch, and window cornices, were made in the late nineteenth century by Col. John Whitford. Whitford, a noted local historian, was the first president of the Atlantic and North Carolina Railroad and a tireless champion of civic improvements in New Bern. Residence of Mr. and Mrs. William F. Ward, Jr.

The living room has a paneled wainscot and a molded cornice with a Wall of Troy band. The room's most distinctive feature is a handsome Georgian mantel with overmantel.

45

**Dr. Forbes' House and Office:** (715-717 Pollock Street).

**House at 726 Pollock Street.** Restored by Mr. and Mrs. E. N. Williams of Greensboro, N. C.

**House at 713 Pollock Street.**

# FEDERAL SIDE-HALL PLAN HOUSES

**Jerkins-Moulton House:** (309 Johnson Street). Traditional brick Federal style house, built ca. 1818. Owned by Captain Thomas Jerkins, a prosperous shipmaster. Alterations made early in this century left intact most of the Federal trim. Owned in the twentieth century by the Moultons, a family of photographers who were famous throughout the state. Residence of Mr. and Mrs. Fred M. Latham.

Intricate Federal window and ceiling molding in the Jerkins-Moulton House.

**William Hatch Bryan House:** (607 Pollock Street). Residence of Dr. and Mrs. Charles Duffy.

**Eli Smallwood House:** (524 East Front Street).
Built ca. 1810 for Eli Smallwood, a prosperous
merchant dealing in the West Indies trade, the
house is a traditional brick side-hall town house,
but is graced with a wealth of elegantly carved
ornament. The front room originally served as
Smallwood's office. Residence of Mrs. D. L. Ward.

This pedimented porch is the most perfectly executed of its type in the city. Note that the transom
uses thin wooden members in imitation of lead.

The sophisticated transverse arch frames the
stair, which carries a stylized wave-pattern brack-
et on each step.

Upstairs bedroom displays a flat-paneled dado
bounded by molded and carved chair rails and
baseboards. Note the elaborate cornice, and above
each window a broken pediment.

The woodwork in the parlor displays the masterful craftsmanship of New Bern's early house carpenters. The mantel itself is plain, but the overmantel is among the most elaborate in the city.

**Jones-Jarvis House:** (528 East Front Street). Frederick Jones, a naval stores merchant, began this brick side-hall plan town house ca. 1810. The interiors were probably finished by Moses Jarvis, also a prosperous merchant, under the direction of builder John Dewey. The house is almost a twin to the Eli Smallwood House next door, and is remarkable for the exceptionally fine carved ornament both inside and out. During the Civil War it became the residence of Union Gen. John Foster. Residence of Dr. and Mrs. William L. Hand.

Detail of transverse arch which provides a visual frame for the stair.

Less ornamented, but still sophisticated second parlor.

**Eubanks House:** (218 Broad Street). Early nineteenth century home built in the Federal style with subsequent additions. Residence of Mrs. Eva F. Bray.

**Eleanor Marshall House:** (227 Eden Street).

**Hendren House:** (227 Change Street). Federal style town house built in the early nineteenth century. Interior woodwork is among the finest remaining in the city. Given to the Historic New Bern Foundation by Centenary United Methodist Church, the house is available for purchase and restoration.

**House at 311 Johnson Street.** Built ca. 1803, enlarged in mid-nineteenth century, and again in 1913. Residence of Mr. and Mrs. O. Haywood Guion.

Detail of pedimented porch.

**House at 211 Broad Street.** Early nineteenth century house near the site of the first printing press in North Carolina, is believed to have been used by James Davis, the colony's first printer. Adaptively restored to serve as the office of the Frank Efird Company.

**Judge Donnell Law Office:** (5105 Trentwood Drive). Typical Federal style office whose interior trim is well preserved. Formerly located in New Bern next to the Donnell House which burned in 1970, the office was moved to its present site and restored by Mr. and Mrs. Julian Warren.

**Isaac Taylor House:** (228 Craven Street). Oldest of the surviving brick, side-hall plan, town houses in New Bern, the house was built in 1792 for Isaac Taylor, a wealthy merchant and ship owner. The house, with three full stories and attic over a basement, is the earliest known use of the Adamesque Federal style architecture in town. Front room was originally an office, accessible only from the street. Residence of Mr. and Mrs. William F. Ward, Sr.

The kitchen with many antique utensils.

Door with original lock box in the drawing room shows some of the house's fine woodwork.

Arches flanking the fireplace are original. The Adamesque mantel, although not original, is an early piece of Federal design.

**Gull Harbor:** (514 East Front Street). Built in the early nineteenth century, this simple Federal style frame house bridges the gap between the elegant Federal mansions of wealthy ship owners and the small cottages of the local artisans and tradesmen. Property of Mrs. C. H. Ashford, Sr.

**House at 231 Change Street.** Residence of Mr. and Mrs. Robert Lee Stallings, Jr.

The dining room of the Stallings' house is elegant in its simplicity.

Beautifully restored second floor bedroom.

**Stevenson House and Office:** (411-415 Craven Street). Traditional early nineteenth century Federal building with later additions. Residence of Mr. and Mrs. Ben O. Jones.

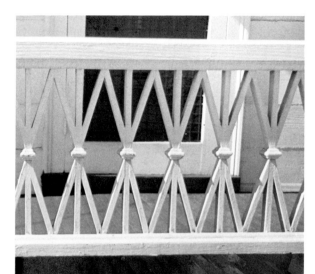

Detail of unique balustrade on Stevenson House porch.

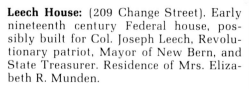

The Stevenson Office adaptively houses the Craven County Board of Election.

**Leech House:** (209 Change Street). Early nineteenth century Federal house, possibly built for Col. Joseph Leech, Revolutionary patriot, Mayor of New Bern, and State Treasurer. Residence of Mrs. Elizabeth R. Munden.

**Lewis Whitehurst House:** (403 Queen Street). Residence of Miss Sadie Whitehurst.

**House at 813 Pollock Street.**

**House at 815 Pollock Street.** Residence of Mr. and Mrs. James R. Laughinghouse.

Unlike other houses of this type, the hall contains no transverse arch.

The interior is very plain and unorthodox for New Bern. The front parlor mantel is Georgian, other ornament is Federal.

**Benjamin Smith House:** (210 Hancock Street). This early version of the brick side-hall plan town house was built ca. 1790. Ground floor is not accessible from the living quarters, suggesting its use as an office or store. Owned by Governor Benjamin Smith, the house combines Georgian and Federal styles. The porch, added in the twentieth century, is probably similar in character to original. Because of its strategic location and view of the river, the house was used by both Confederate and Federal troops during the Civil War to guard the railroad bridge across the Trent River.

Entrance porch and transom above the door are classic examples of the artistry of New Bern's early craftsmen.

**Bryan House and Office:** (603-605 Pollock Street). The house was built 1803-1804 by architect Martin Stevenson, Sr., for James Bryan, a prominent merchant, as a traditional New Bern side-hall plan town house distinguished by fine carved ornament. Later, mid-nineteenth century alterations include Greek Revival white marble mantels, silver doorknobs, locks, and hinges, and sliding doors in the parlors. Residence of Dr. and Mrs. Charles Ashford, Jr.

The Federal style office was built ca. 1820 by United States Congressman John Herritage Bryan.

Dining room with Federal style woodwork.

Silver door embellishment.

**Old City Hall:** (220-226 Craven Street). Turn of the century facade hides early nineteenth century town houses.

**Headmaster's House:** (442 Johnson Street). Quaint cottage, soon to be restored by Mr. and Mrs. Paul Crayton.

**House at 223 Craven Street.** Early town house now houses modern business.

**Harvey Mansion:** (219 Tryon Palace Drive). Built between 1804 and 1816, this three story building over a full basement included home, office, and warehouse facilities for merchant John Harvey, whose other wharves and warehouses were located on the Trent River. Interiors are finished with fine Adamesque mantels and woodwork, probably the work of John Hay, a noted carriage and furniture maker.

Impressive door in ballroom with elegant Federal overdoor.

Second floor ballroom was the grandest room in early nineteenth century New Bern as is indicated by this highly ornamented and sophisticated locally-made mantel.

**Masonic Temple and Theater:** (516 Hancock Street). Built 1802-1809 by St. John's Lodge No. 3, A.F. & A.M., which was organized before 1764 and chartered in 1772. The building was designed by John Dewey. The theater on the first floor has been in continuous use as a theater since 1804. The lodge room on the second floor contains the fine original Federal style woodwork. The walls of the lodge room were painted ca. 1847 in *trompe l'oeil* symbols of Masonry by an itinerant artist. The ceiling, representing a celestial atmosphere, shows the "All Seeing Eye," the sun, moon, stars, and Jacob's Ladder, which, according to Masonic ritual, can be ascended by devoting one's life to faith, hope, and charity.

# FEDERAL CENTRAL-HALL PLAN HOUSES

**Attmore-Oliver House:** (513 Broad Street). The house was built as a one-and-one-half story cottage ca. 1790 by Samuel Chapman, merchant and clerk of Superior Court of Craven County, 1788-1806. Isaac Taylor remodeled the house in 1834 for his daughter. The house was restored in the early 1950s by the New Bern Historical Society to its 1834 appearance. The street fascade, with a fine Greek Revival Doric entrance porch and balconies beneath full-length windows, contrasts with the two-story porch in the rear. The four exterior end chimneys are unusual in the city. The interiors are Federal in form but use Greek Revival moldings. The Attmore-Oliver House is maintained by and serves as the headquarters for the New Bern Historical Society.

**Tisdale-Jones House:** (520 New Street). Earliest part of the house was built by Robert Palmer ca. 1769, who came to New Bern to assume his seat on the colonial Superior Court bench. Later purchased by loyalist Martin Howard, Chief-Justice of the colony, and first Grand Master of the Masonic Lodge of North Carolina. William Tisdale acquired the house in 1776. Tisdale, who probably added the front section of the house, was a member of the Assembly, the Provincial Congress, New Bern Committee of Safety, and Judge of the Admiralty Court. He was a silversmith, and was employed to engrave the Great Seal of the state in 1778. The House was owned, 1796-1798, by Francis Xavier Martin, jurist, publisher, and historian; 1798-1812, by John Louis Taylor, first Justice of the North Carolina Supreme Court; and by Asa Jones, wealthy planter and shipper. House is now adaptively used as offices by the New Bern Board of Education.

**First New Bern Academy Building.** (514 New Street). The academy was chartered in 1764. The first building, built in 1766, burned in 1795. Present building was completed in 1806. Governor Tryon wrote the Earl of Shelburne that this school was "the first established in this province by legislative authority." Design of the building was probably provided by James Coor. The exterior is Georgian in form, but the interiors display academic Federal woodwork and mantels, which are remarkably intact. The building served continuously as a school until 1972, except for four years during the Union occupation when it was used as a hospital.

**Simpson-Oaksmith-Patterson House:**
(226 East Front Street). Built ca. 1810
by merchant Samuel Simpson, the
building began as a brick, two-story,
center-hall plan, Federal era house.
Between 1884 and 1887 a mansard-roof
tower with sculptured heads, stuccoed
string courses and imaginative dormers were added. In 1887 it won the
title "Greatest Architectural Curiosi-
ty of the South." The house was used
as the Provost Marshall's office and
Guard House during the Union occupation in the Civil War. Vance Academy, a boarding and day school, operat-
ed here during the 1870s and 1880s. Unfortunately destroyed while this book
was in publication.

Sculptured heads of a man and two
lions are unique in New Bern.

**McLin-Hancock House:** (507 Middle Street). This early nineteenth century coastal cottage with Federal interiors stands out because of its strict symmetry. Probably built by Thomas McLin, a
coppersmith and merchant.

Black marble mantel in front parlor of the Hatch-Washington House.

**Hatch-Washington House:** (216 Pollock Street). Built ca. 1818-1819 by Durand Hatch, Jr., and finished or renovated by John Washington ca. 1827. The plan and woodwork are very different from that usually found in the city. Adaptively restored as the "Henderson House Restaurant."

**Vail-Clarke House:** (519 East Front Street). Early nineteenth century Federal coastal style cottage with double porches front and rear is similar to those built in Beaufort, N. C. The house was built by Jeremiah Vail, an influential politician. Later the house was occupied by Mary Bayard Clarke, noted poetess. Residence of Miss Celia M. Lively.

**Mitchell-Bryan House:** (211 Johnson Street). The house was built ca. 1800 as a side-hall plan Federal house. The right side was added ca. 1807 in the same style. The entrance porch was remodeled ca. 1850 in Greek Revival style. Residence of Mr. George Allen Ives, Sr.

The "dog trot" or breezeway connects the separate kitchen at the rear of the house.

**Oliver House:** (512 East Front Street). This early nineteenth century Federal style house has a gambrel roof, unusual in New Bern. Residence of Mrs. Charles H. Ashford, Sr.

The interiors of the Oliver House are simple, but elegant.

House at 206 Metcalf Street.

House at 206 Change Street.

House at 309 Bern Street.

House at 501 New Street.

House at 718 Pollock Street.

**Silas Latham House:** (816 Pollock Street).

**House at 812 Pollock Street.**

**House at 803 Pollock Street.**

**House at 819 Pollock Street.**

**House at 823 Pollock Street.**

**James Bright House:** (514 Craven Street). This small, late eighteenth century cottage, was recently moved to this location and restored by Dr. and Mrs. W. F. Evans.

Dining room of the Bright House.

Exterior door retains the original HL hinges in the Bright House.

**Clark House:** (419 Metcalf Street). This late eighteenth century gambrel roof house was once used as a school. Residence of Mrs. Isabelle Taylor.

# FEDERAL TRANSITIONAL HOUSES

**William Hollister House:** (613 Broad Street). This frame side-hall plan Federal style house is the last full application of the style in New Bern. The house was built in 1840-1841 for William Hollister, a wealthy merchant. Residence of Mrs. Helen Hollister Swan.

Federal style transverse arch frames the stair which displays wave pattern brackets on each step.

Interior uses some Greek Revival era elements, but the Federal style dominates, being executed in mid-nineteenth century materials.

Detail of the delicate cast iron railings on porch steps.

The black marble mantels in the Justice House.

**Justice House:** (221 East Front Street). This large, brick, town house was completed before 1842. The porch was added in the twentieth century. Residence of Mrs. Eliza E. Turner.

**Alexander Miller House and Store:** (415 Broad Street).

**House at 620 Craven Street.** Residence of Mrs. Bessie H. Eagle.

**House at 820 Broad Street.** Residence of Misses Rachel and Ellen Hancock.

**Benjamin Ellis House:** (215 Pollock Street). Residence of Mr. Gerald Colvin.

**House at 227 East Front Street.**

**House at 208 Johnson Street.** Residence of Mr. and Mrs. W. B. Pugh, Jr.

**Dr. Smallwood's House and Office:** (501-505 Craven Street). Residence of Miss Lucile Meredith.

Stair of Dr. Smallwood's House.

Black marble fireplace of Smallwood's House.

Dr. Smallwood's Office.

**Jerkins-Bryan House:** (520 Craven Street). Built by Captain Thomas Jerkins ca. 1830, the house displays Greek Revival interior trim on a traditional Federal plan and exterior.

Widow's Walk atop the Jerkins-Bryan House.

**Sparrow-Daniels House:** (222 East Front Street). This massive, three story town house is one of an elite group of only seven brick side-hall houses remaining in New Bern. The exterior bears a strong resemblance to the Isaac Taylor House on Craven Street. The robust quality of the Greek Revival elements inside are unrivaled in the city.

**Primrose House:** (318 Craven Street). This house, transitional in style between the Federal and Greek Revival styles, is adaptively maintained for lawyers' offices by Mr. and Mrs. Lloyd Gilliken.

**Jerkins-Duffy House:** (301 Johnson Street). Built by Captain Thomas Jerkins in the 1830s, the house is Federal in style with some Greek Revival elements on the inside. Former residence of Mrs. Richard (Minnete) Duffy, an early leader in the movement to rebuild Tryon Palace. Residence of Mr. and Mrs. Clarence B. Beasley.

# ECLECTIC HOUSES

**Ulysses S. Mace House:** (518 Broad Street). This fine late Italianate style house was built ca. 1884. Residence of Mrs. W. B. Wadsworth.

The unusual stair in the Mace House begins in the middle of the hall and curves around to join the wall.

**Stimson House:** (605 East Front Street).

**Foy-Munger House:** (516 Middle Street). Residence of Mrs. Paul W. Mengel.

**Judge Manly House:** (515 East Front Street). Residence of Mr. and Mrs. John Tull Hollister, Jr.

**Senator Simmons House:** (415 East Front Street). Residence of Mr. and Mrs. Harvey J. Paquette.

**Slover-Bradham House:** (201 Johnson Street). George Slover, a wealthy merchant, built this house ca. 1848 in the Renaissance Revival style. The strict symmetry of the facade focuses attention on the front entrance, whose door contains the original hardware, including a brass lock box and pendant handles on both sides. The house was used during the Civil War Occupation by Gen. Ambrose Burnside as the Headquarters of the Eighteenth Army Corps and the Federal Department of North Carolina. Later owned by C. D. Bradham, who invented "Pepsi-Cola" in his drugstore at Pollock and Middle Streets in 1898. This most unique structure, the "best executed, most sophisticated example of Renaissance Revival architecture in the state" is now the residence of Mr. and Mrs. Lawrence A. Stith.

Delicate iron railings enhance the continuous balconies beneath the first floor windows.

Slover lavishly decorated the interior with marble mantels, porcelain and silver escutcheons, and silver hinges and door knobs in the parlor.

**Slover-Bradham House Dependency:** (521 East Front Street). Nineteenth century kitchen and slave quarters for the Slover-Bradham House. Residence of Mr. C. W. Bynum.

**Hollowell House:** (614 Middle Street). Residence of Mr. and Mrs. Michael Brantley.

**Rhem-Waldrop House.** (701 Broad Street). Handsome Renaissance Revival structure was built ca. 1850 by George Attmore. For many years it was the home of Joseph Rhem, a wealthy merchant. Adaptively restored by Mr. John A. Clark, Jr.

**Street House:** (509 Pollock Street). Residence of Miss Mary P. Ward.

**Mitchell House:** (212 Tryon Palace Drive). Residence of Mrs. T. J. Mitchell.

**Wade House:** (214 Tryon Palace Drive). This house was built in the early nineteenth century and remodeled before 1885 when mansard roof was added. Note cast iron roof cresting. Residence of Mrs. Cedric Boyd.

Detail of side porch on Wade House.

House at 310 New Street.

House at 516 Johnson Street.

House at 616-618 East Front Street.

**Thomas Jerkins House:** (305 Johnson Street). Built ca. 1849 by prosperous ship owner, Thomas Jerkins, the house, of Italianate design, is one of the earliest surviving houses to depart from the Federal style, but retains the side-hall plan. Residence of Mr. and Mrs. C. Walker Hodges, Jr.

View of the rear of the Jerkins House.

Stair in the Jerkins House.

Dignified, but comfortable dining room.

**Edward R. Stanly House:** (502 Pollock Street). Built ca. 1850 by the wealthy manufacturer, Edward R. Stanly (no relation to the John Wright Stanly family), in the Renaissance Revival style, the house retains the favored side-hall plan. Owned and adaptively restored by New Bern architect Robert H. Stephens, the building now houses the Neuse River Council of Governments.

Wooden porch was added in the twentieth century.

Detail of stair and pressed tin wainscot.

**Edward R. Stanly House Dependency:** (301 Hancock Street). Built ca. 1850, the dependency now houses the "Ward House" interior decorating store.

**Carpenter Gothic Barn:** (218 Metcalf Street).

Detail of eaves.

**Roberts House:** (501 Metcalf Street). Residence of Mrs. Mary N. Roberts.

**House at 408 Hancock Street.**

**Former First Baptist Parsonage:** (304 Johnson Street).

Detail of eaves.

**House at 224 Pollock Street.** Residence of Mrs. Bradley C. Duffy.

**House at 207 Pollock Street.**

Detail of intricate exterior wood-work.

**George Slover House:** (209 Johnson Street). The unique mixing of Queen Anne and Shingle styles in this house produces a fascinating, eclectic result. Residence of Mr. and Mrs. R. D. Baskervill.

Massive newel post in the Slover House.

Cozy arched bay window in the Slover House.

**Harvey Wadsworth House:** (515 Broad Street). Alone of its type in New Bern, the house is distinguished by beautifully leaded windows that mark the front entrance. Residence of Mrs. Harvey Wadsworth.

# QUEEN ANNE
# STYLE HOUSES

**W. B. Blades House:** (602 Middle Street). Built in 1903, the house was designed by New Bern architect Herbert W. Simpson for lumber, banking, and manufacturing magnate, W. B. Blades. The thirty-eight room house, in the Queen Anne Style verging on Neo-Classical Revival, is a fantastic combination of turrets, bow and bay windows, round-headed and circular dormers, and paneled chimney stacks. Mr. Blades' own lumber company provided the pine, mahogany, oak, and birds-eye maple used in the house. The dining room is finished in carved oak and features a built-in cupboard and chimney piece with paneled overmantel. The stair-hall features a medieval style chimney piece with a massive brick fireplace. The house displays at every turn remarkably refined craftsmanship, especially in wood. Residence of Mrs. W. B. Blades.

**Jarvis House.** (220 Pollock Street). Residence of Mr. Parkhill Jarvis.

**Foy House.** (512 Middle Street).

# NEO-CLASSICAL STYLE HOUSES

**C. S. Hollister House:** (614 Craven Street). Residence of
Mr. Charles S. Hollister, Jr.

**L. I. Moore House:** (511 East Front Street). Residence
of Dr. and Mrs. R. A. Moore.

Newel post and delicate stair.

Beautifully decorated black marble fireplace and mantel.

**House at 516 Pollock Street:** This house ca. 1882, remodeled in the early twentieth century, was built in the Neo-Classical Revival style. Residence of Mr. and Mrs. Paul Cox.

Elaborate ceiling molding.

Dining room testifies to tasteful living.

# GOVERNMENT BUILDINGS

**United States Post Office and Court House:** (413 Middle Street). Completed in 1935 on the original site of the John Wright Stanly House, the building was considered extravagant for the needs of the city at that time. The murals in the Court Room depict significant events in New Bern's history.

The First Provincial Congress, August 25-27, 1774.

In 1787, Judges Samuel Spencer, Samuel Ashe, and John Williams heard the case of Bayard v. Singleton, in which the state court ruled an act of the legislature unconstitutional. This ruling, the first by an American court, helped establish the principal that the legislature is limited in its power by the constitution, now considered a fundamental principal of American law.

The center panel above the Judge's desk depicts two scenes: a) Baron de Graffenried recruiting settlers to migrate with him to the New World; and b) James Davis and the first printing press in North Carolina which Davis brought with him in 1749 when he settled in New Bern.

**City Hall:** (300 Pollock Street). This imposing Romanesque Revival style building was built 1895-1897, and served as the United States Post Office, Court House, and Customs House until 1936 when the new Federal Building was completed. The building has served as New Bern's municipal building since then. The unique richness and appeal of the structure is achieved through the use of contrasting colors, textures, and shapes. The high foundation is in rusticated pink granite; the first story in red pressed brick; the second and third stories in buffed pressed brick. The four-faced clock tower was added in 1910. The cast iron black bears above the entrances were gifts from, and are symbolic of Berne, Switzerland. The interior retains much of the original woodwork. Especially remarkable is the stair and its massive newel post. The courtroom displays its original trim and furniture.

City Hall ca. 1900, before the tower was added.

**Craven County Court House:** (300 Broad Street).

Governor's Boulder on the Court House lawn honors three North Carolina Governors who came from New Bern, Richard Dobbs Spaight, Richard Dobbs Spaight, Jr., and Abner Nash.

The original entrance was on Craven Street.

# HISTORIC CHURCHES

**First Presbyterian Church:** (412 New Street). Built 1819-1822 by Uriah Sandy, this Federal style church is reminiscent of New England churches and is unique in North Carolina. The congregation was organized in 1817. The symmetry of the exterior is repeated inside the foyer with a pair of transverse arches and spiral stairs, and in the auditorium. The church was used as a hospital during the Civil War Occupation.

Detail of excellently executed tetra-style pedimented Ionic portico.

View of interior from rear showing balconies and chandelier.

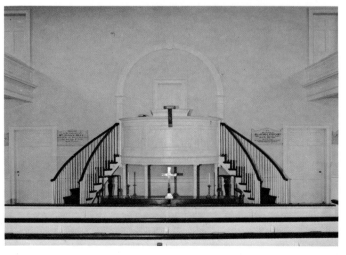

The raised pulpit was carefully and scholarly restored in 1936.

The Stick Style porch was added to the base of the tower in 1884.

**Christ Episcopal Church:** (320 Pollock Street). Christ Church Parish was formed in 1741 out of Craven Parish, formed in 1715. The foundations of the first church building, 1750, are preserved in a corner of the church yard. The present Gothic Revival building was built in 1875, incorporating the brick shell that remained after an 1871 fire which gutted the previous church which had been built in 1824. The tower did not exist on the original structure. The cemetery in the church yard contains some of the oldest graves in the city, including that of Revolutionary patriot John Wright Stanly; James Reed, the church's first rector; and Charles Elliot, attorney general of the colony. The Parish House, 1904-1908, was designed by Herbert W. Simpson.

The heavy, dark wooden trim contrasts strongly with the white plaster walls.

Detail of communion rail and intricately carved altar.

**First Baptist Church:** (239 Middle Street). The congregation was first organized in 1809, although Baptists were present in New Bern as early as 1740. The present Gothic Revival style structure was built in 1848, and was designed by Thomas and Son of New York. President Harry Truman attended services here six days after defeating Thomas Dewey in 1948. Among the many prominent ministers to serve this congregation were: William Hooper, a founder of Wake Forest University; Samuel Wait, the first President of Wake Forest University; Thomas Meredith, for whom Meredith College was named; Richard Furman, for whom Furman University was named; and Martin R. Forey, founder of Chowan College. First Baptist began publication of *Biblical Recorder* in 1835, and it continues to be the official publication of the North Carolina Baptist Convention.

First Baptist Church, ca. 1890.

Detail of balcony.

The church today.

**St. Paul's Roman Catholic Church:** (510 Middle Street). The oldest Catholic congregation in North Carolina was established in 1824. This Federal style structure is the oldest Catholic church in the state. The exterior remains essentially as designed in 1839 by Bishop England of the Diocese of Charleston.

Above the altar hangs William Joseph Williams' painting, "Jesus on the Cross", ca. 1821.

Detail of the Greek Revival style steeple added in 1896.

**Centenary United Methodist Church:** (416 Middle Street). The present structure built in 1904-1905, is a turreted mass of irregular projections, a late example of Romantic Eclecticism, combining the styles of Romanesque and Chateausque revivals. The original building was designed by Herbert W. Simpson. The Congregation was established in 1722. Although no Methodist church building existed here until the nineteenth century, George Whitefield preached in New Bern in 1739.

The interior was sympathetically remodeled in 1965 by Robert H. Stephens of New Bern which "further dramatized the already fluid space produced by the juxtaposition of wall space and roof planes."

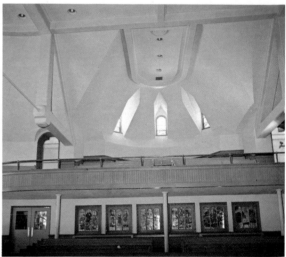

View of rear of auditorium and balcony.

Intimate chapel off the main auditorium.

**First Church of Christ, Scientist:** (406 Middle Street). Congregation established in 1902 by Mary Hatch Harrison, the first of this denomination in North Carolina. The Neo-Classical Revival, temple form structure was designed by Herbert W. Simpson.

Ionic tetrastyle pedimented portico.

Above the tall Classical Revival mantel is one of the four inscriptions on the walls of the church furnished in 1907 by Mary Baker Eddy, the Discoverer and Founder of Christian Science.

Interior of the church, for which Mrs. Eddy donated $3,000 to the building fund.

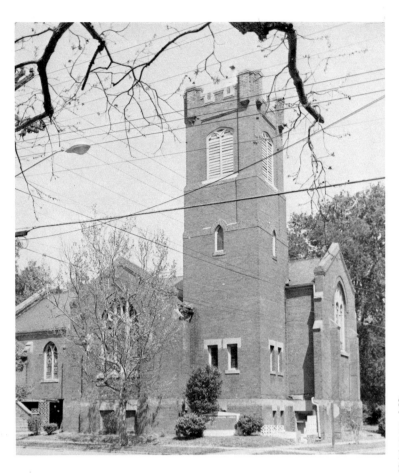

**St. Cyprian's Episcopal Church:** (613 Queen Street).
The first Baptist church building ca. 1812, was
located on this site. That early chapel was given
to the free Negro congregation in 1848 when the
Baptists erected their present building on Middle
Street. This church was built in 1907-1913.

**Temple B'nai Sholem:** (505 Middle Street). This Neo-Classical Revival Temple, based on plans designed by Herbert W. Simpson, was completed in 1908. The congregation was established before 1824.

Detail of pedimented portico.

The focal point of the Temple is the Ark containing the Torah.

**Broad Street Christian Church:** (802 Broad Street).

The massive themes of the exterior are continued in the interior of the church.

# CEMETERIES

**Cedar Grove Cemetery:** (602 Queen Street). Cedar Grove was begun by Christ Church as a cemetery in 1800, with many earlier graves reinterred here. The older section is well landscaped, with the later expansion being laid out in a park-like fashion. The cemetery was transferred to the City in 1853. At that time the wall and triple-arched gateway were built, and are among the best examples of the use of marl. Some of the best early markers are simple horizontal slabs raised about a foot above the ground on brick walls. A later more sophisticated version elevates the slabs on six urn-shaped balusters.

Cedar Grove contains the graves of New Bern's most famous citizens and is notable for well designed funerary art and fine ironwork. When the City assumed control of the cemetery, Dr. Francis Lister Hawks composed this verse: "Still hallowed be this spot where lies/ Each dear loved one in earth's embrace/ Our God their treasured dust doth prize/ Man should protect their resting place."

Confederate Memorial.

**National Cemetery:** (1711 National Avenue). Burials began here during the Civil War Occupation, 1862-1865. Cemetery contains the graves of Union soldiers from twenty states.

Monument erected by Massachusetts to honor that state's Civil War soldiers who died in the Department of North Carolina.

**Hebrew Cemetery:** (1707 National Avenue). This quiet, shaded cemetery contains tombstones inscribed in both English and Hebrew.

**Spaight Family Cemetery:** (Madam Moore's Lane). Located across the Neuse River on the former "Clermont Plantation," this cemetery contains the remains of Richard Spaight, 1730-1763; "Madame" Mary Vail Moore, 1705-1764; Gov. Richard Dobbs Spaight, 1758-1802; Mary Jones Leech, 1765-1810; William Wilson Spaight, 1794-1812; Charles George Spaight, 1798-1831; Gov. Richard Dobbs Spaight, Jr., 1796-1850; Margaret Elizabeth Spaight, 1800-1831; Margaret Elizabeth Donnell, 1828-1836; Col. Joseph Leech, 1720-1803; Mary Dorothy Vail, 1735-1775.

**Greenwood Cemetery:** (800 Cypress Street). These are the oldest tombstones in this Negro cemetery.

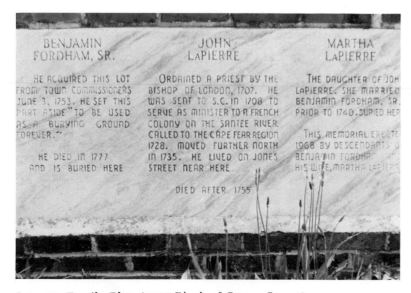

**Jennette Family Plot:** (1100 Block of Queen Street).

# POINTS OF INTEREST

**Second New Bern Academy Building:** (517 Hancock Street). Although built in 1884-1885, the overall design blends well with the earlier Academy Building.

**Baxter Clock:** (323 Pollock Street). Installed in 1920, this Seth Thomas Street Clock with four faces, is the only one of its type to have survived in North Carolina, and apparently one of only three still operating in the country.

**Cypress Tree:** (520 East Front Street). One of twenty trees in the Hall of Fame of American Trees.

**All Saints Chapel:** (809 Pollock Street).

**Former First Citizens Bank:** (317 Middle Street).

**North Carolina National Bank:** (313 Pollock Street).

**Building at 219-221 Craven Street.**

**Elks Temple:** (400 Pollock Street).

**Green and Redmond Store:** (405 Broad Street).

**Hotel Albert:** (224-226 Middle Street).

**House at 220 Middle Street.**

**House and Store at 606 East Front Street.**

**Shoemasters:** (246 Middle Street).

**Atlantic and East Carolina Railway Station:** (416 Queen Street).

**Firemen's Museum:** (420 Broad Street). The purpose of the Firemen's Museum is to preserve historical fire fighting relics and records, and to immortalize those brave men who started and built the New Bern Fire Department. The Atlantic Hook and Ladder Company was the City's first chartered fire fighting organization, being chartered on May 14, 1845. The New Berne Steam Fire Engine Company, No. 1, was organized here January 1, 1865 by Union soldiers who later stayed on after the war. This company has been called the "Button Company" ever since the City purchased a Button fire engine in 1884. The Atlantic and Button companies competed vigorously over the years as the volunteers increased their effectiveness. In 1900 the Button company set two world records that still stand: first, for producing standing quick steam in one minute forty-six seconds; and for producing running quick steam in two minutes twelve seconds.

The Firemen's Museum, which contains antique fire engines and numerous other relics, is open Tuesday thru Saturday, 9:30-12, 1-5; and Sunday, 1-5; closed holidays. Free parking is available at the rear of 418 Broad Street while visiting the museum.

The Button Steamer was purchased by the city in 1884.

The Atlantic Steamer, built by the Silsby Company, was in continuous service from 1879 to 1915.

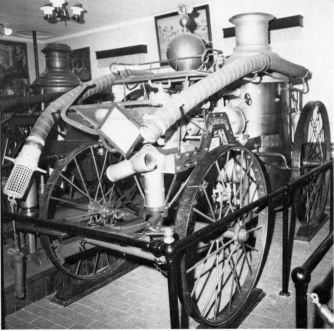

BICENTENNIAL MEDALLION. The Bicentennial Medallion was issued by the New Bern/Craven County American Revolution Bicentennial Commission as the official souvenir of the Bicentennial Festival commemorating the two hundredth anniversary of the First Provincial Congress. Miss Janet Latham of New Bern designed the medallion. The Barco Mint of New Orleans, Inc. manufactured them in Pure Silver (.999 Fine), Bronze, and Aluminum. The medallion was minted in the following numbers: 2,665 Bronze; 1,142 Silver; 13 Gold Plated on Silver. In addition the Bicentennial Commission distributed fifteen thousand gold anodized aluminum medallions—one for each school student in Craven County.

# INDEX

# STREET ADDRESS GUIDE

**BERN STREET**
#309, House, 66

**BROAD STREET**
#211, House, 51
#218, Eubanks House, 50
#300, Court House, 91
#405, Green and Redmond Store, 105
#415, Alexander Miller House and Store, 70
#420, Firemen's Museum, 107
#513, Attmore-Oliver House, 61
#515, Harvey Wadsworth House, 84
#518, U. S. Mace House, 74
#613, William Hollister House, 69
#701, Rhem-Waldrop House, 77
#802, Broad Street Christian Church, 100
#820, House, 71

**CHANGE STREET**
#206, House, 66
#209, Leech House, 54
#227, Hendren House, 50
#231, House, 53

**CRAVEN STREET**
#219-221, House, 105
#220-226, Old City Hall, 58
#223, House, 58
#228, Isaac Taylor House, 52
#307, Judge Gaston Law Office, 42
#318, Primrose House, 73
#411-415, Stevenson House and Office, 42
#421, Coor-Gaston House, 44
#501-505, Dr. Smallwood's House and Office, 72
#506, Smith-Whitford House, 45
#514, James Bright House, 68
#520, Jerkins-Bryan House, 72
#614, C. S. Hollister House, 87
#620, House, 71

**CYPRESS STREET**
#800, Greenwood Cemetery, 103

**EAST FRONT STREET**
#220, Justice House, 70
#222, Sparrow-Daniels House, 73
#226, Simpson-Oaksmith-Patterson House, 63
#227, House, 71
#415, Senator Simmons House, 75
#501, Coor-Bishop House, 41
#511, L. I. Moore House, 87
#512, Oliver House, 65
#514, Gull Harbor, 53
#515, Judge Manly House, 75
#519, Vail-Clarke House, 64
#520, Cypress Tree, 104
#521, Slover-Bradham House Dependency, 77
#524, Eli Smallwood House, 48
#528, Jones-Jarvis House, 49
#605, Stimson House, 74
#606, House, 106
#616-618, House, 79

**EDEN STREET**
#227, Eleanor Marshall House, 50
#231, Jones House, 34

**GEORGE STREET**
#307, John Wright Stanly House, 36
#313, Major James Daves House, 39

**HANCOCK STREET**
#210, Benjamin Smith House, 56
#213, York-Gordon House, 43
#217, House, 42
#301, Edward R. Stanly House Dependency, 81
#306, Hawks House, 39
#408, House, 82
#516, Masonic Temple and Theater, 60
#517, Second New Bern Academy Building, 104

**JOHNSON STREET**
#201, Slover-Bradham House, 76
#208, House, 71
#209, George Slover House, 84
#211, Mitchell-Bryan House, 65
#213, Brinson House, 42
#301, Jerkins-Duffy House, 73
#304, Former First Baptist Parsonage, 83
#305, Thomas Jerkins House, 80
#309, Jerkins-Moulton House, 47
#311, House, 51
#442, Headmaster's House, 58
#516, House, 79

**METCALF STREET**
#206, House, 66
#218, Carpenter's Gothic Barn, 82
#419, Clark House, 68
#501, Roberts House, 82

**MIDDLE STREET**
#220, House, 106
#224-226, Hotel Albert, 106
#239, First Baptist Church, 94
#246, Shoemaster's, 106
#317, Former First Citizens Bank, 105
#406, First Church of Christ, Scientist, 97
#413, Post Office, 89
#416, Centenary United Methodist Church, 96
#505, Temple Chester B'nai Sholem, 99
#507, McLin-Hancock House, 63
#510, St. Paul's Roman Catholic Church, 95
#512, Foy House, 86
#516, Foy-Munger House, 75
#602, W. B. Blades House, 85
#614, Hollowell House, 77
#616, Elijah Clark House, 42

**NATIONAL AVENUE**
#1707, Hebrew Cemetery, 102
#1711, National Cemetery, 102

**NEW STREET**
#214, Coor-Bishop House Dependency, 41
#219, Mary Hatch Harrison House, 43
#310, House, 79
#412, First Presbyterian Church, 92
#501, House, 66
#514, First New Bern Academy Building, 62
#520, Tisdale-Jones House, 62

**POLLOCK STREET**
#207, House, 83
#215, Benjamin Ellis House, 71
#216, Hatch-Washington House, 64
#220, Jarvis House, 86
#224, House, 83
#300, City Hall, 90
#313, North Carolina National Bank, 105
#320, Christ Episcopal Church, 93

## PHOTO CREDITS

BOB JONES, New Bern: pages 8, 34 (Jones House), 38, 40, 41, 42, 43 (Mary Hatch Harrison House), 44, 45, 46, 47 (Jerkins-Moulton House), 48, 49, 50 (Hendren House), 51, 52, 53, 54 (Stevenson House and Office, exteriors), 55 (Houses at 813 and 815 Pollock Street), 56, 57 (Bryan House and Office, interiors and Office), 58, 59 (Harvey Mansion, exteriors), 60, 61, 63 (McLin-Hancock House), 64, 65, 68, 69, 70 (A. Miller House and Store), 71 (Benjamin Ellis House and House at 820 Broad Street), 72, 73, 76, 77, 78 (Street House), 79, 80, 81, 82 (Carpenter Gothic Barn, detail of eaves, and Roberts House), 83 (Houses at 207 and 224 Pollock Street), 84, 85, 86, 88, 89, 90 (City Hall, exterior trim), 91, 92, 93, 94 (First Baptist Church, interiors), 95 (St. Paul's Roman Catholic Church, interiors), 96, 97 (First Church of Christ, Scientist, interiors and front exterior), 98, 99 (Temple B'nai Sholem, interior) 100, 101, 102, 103, 104 (Cypress Tree), 105, 106, 107, and cover photographs.

TONY P. WRENN, courtesy of the North Carolina Division of Archives and History, Raleigh: pages 39 (Hawks House, interior), 47 (William Hatch Bryan House), 50 (Eleanor Marshall House), 54 (Stevenson House, detail of balustrade), 59 (Harvey Mansion, interiors), 63 (Simpson-Oaksmith-Patterson House, detail of tower), 66, 67, 70 (Justice House, detail of railing), 71 (Houses at 620 Craven Street, 227 East Front Street, and 208 Johnson Street), 74 (Mace House), 75, 78 (Mitchell House), 82 (House at 408 Hancock Street and Carpenter Gothic Barn, exterior), 83 (Former First Baptist Parsonage), 87, 95 (St. Paul's Roman Catholic Church, exterior), 97 (First Church of Christ, Scientist, side exterior), 99 (Temple B'nai Sholem, detail of pediment), 104 (All Saints Chapel).

STUART C. SCHWARTZ, courtesy of the North Carolina Division of Archives and History, Raleigh: pages 39 (Hawks House, exterior), 43 (York-Gordon House), 50 (Eubanks House), 55 (Lewis Whitehurst House), 70 (Justice House, exterior), 78 (Wade House), exterior), 90 (City Hall, exterior with tower), 104 (Baxter Clock).

TONY VAUGHN, courtesy of the North Carolina Division of Archives and History, Raleigh: pages 39 (Major James Daves House), 62, 63 (Simpson-Oaksmith-Patterson House, exterior), 74 (Stimson House), 94 (First Baptist Church, exterior), 99 (Temple B'nai Sholem, exterior), 104 (Second New Bern Academy Building).

JANET K. SEAPKER, courtesy of the North Carolina Division of Archives and History: pages 57 (Bryan House, exterior), 70 (Justice House, fireplace), 78 (Wade House, detail of porch), 95 (St. Paul's Roman Catholic Church, detail of steeple).

CHARLES BAPTIE, Annondale, Virginia: pages 33, 37 (Latham Garden).

HERB REA, Tryon Palace, New Bern: pages 36, 37 (Kellenberger Garden and Green Garden).

DR. CHARLES ASHFORD, JR., New Bern: page 57 (Detail of porch).

BENNERS STUDIO, New Bern: pages, 34 (McKinlay-Daves House), 35.

GEROCK STUDIO, courtesy of the New Bern Historical Society: page 90 (City Hall, ca. 1903).

B. VON HUFF, courtesy of the North Carolina Museum of Natural History: page 94 (First Baptist Church, ca. 1890).

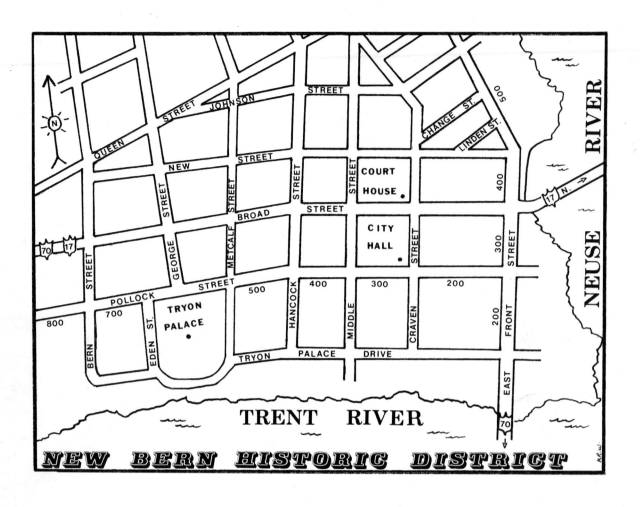

NEW BERN HISTORIC DISTRICT

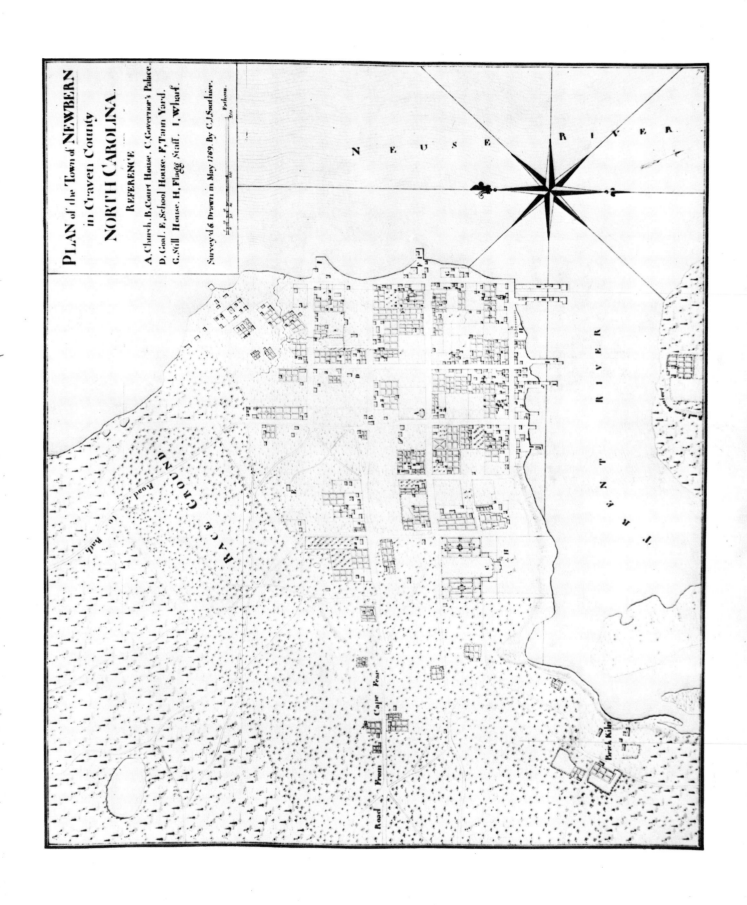

# PLAN of the Town of NEWBERN
in Craven County
## NORTH CAROLINA.
### REFERENCE.

A. Church. B. Court House. C. Governor's Palace.
D. Goal. E. School House. F. Town Yard.
G. Still House. H. Flagg Staff. I. Wharf.

Survey'd & Drawn in May 1769. By C.J.Sauthier.

NEUSE RIVER

TRENT RIVER

RACE GROUND

Road to the Bath

Road From Cape Fear

Brick Kiln